University Press of New England ❧ Hanover and London

MASTER POTTER

in the GARDEN

Guy Wolff

Suzanne Staubach

Photographs by Joseph Szalay

University Press of New England

www.upne.com

© 2013 Suzanne Staubach

All rights reserved

Manufactured in the United States of America

Designed by Mindy Basinger Hill

For permission to reproduce any of the
material in this book, contact Permissions,
University Press of New England, One
Court Street, Suite 250, Lebanon NH 03766;
or visit www.upne.com

Library of Congress Cataloging-in-Publication Data

Staubach, Suzanne.

Guy Wolff: master potter in the garden /
Suzanne Staubach ; photographs by Joseph Szalay.

          pages   cm

Includes bibliographical references and index.

ISBN 978-1-61168-366-0 (pbk.: alk. paper) —
ISBN 978-1-61168-403-2 (ebook)

1. Pottery craft. 2. Flowerpots. 3. Wolff, Guy. I. Title.

TT920 S726 2013

738.1′2—dc23   2012049017

5   4   3   2   1

THIS BOOK IS FOR

ALL MY FRIENDS WITH

THEIR HANDS IN MUD,

BE THEY POTTERS,

GARDENERS OR BOTH

CONTENTS

Suzanne Staubach has written *Guy Wolff: Master Potter in the Garden*, a book about a man who chose to be a potter. He seemed to know, even as a young child, that this would be the path he would take in life.

Guy loves pottery with a passion, with dedication, and with an intense focus as he leads the life of a full-time studio potter. As such, he has had much recognition and enjoyed continued success in making, selling, and living with his pottery.

His work "reclaims the notion that thrilling and beautiful form can still emerge out of the realm of the practical" (Paul Goldberger). Aesthetically and philosophically, he has developed his work around the idea of bringing together the old and the new. Although tradition is a vital part of his expression, his pottery is also about his personal interpretation of making useful pottery fit into one's daily life. He has spent his life working very hard at something that continues to fascinate him. We can all benefit from such dedication.

As Philip Rawson has said: "The pot fills the gap between art and life."

Congratulations to Suzy Staubach for bringing Guy Wolff, a rare and special talent, to all who read her book.

Val Cushing ✥ PROFESSOR EMERITUS
SCHOOL OF ART & DESIGN, NYS COLLEGE OF CERAMICS,
ALFRED UNIVERSITY

I can't remember how I first met Guy. Maybe we were both attending the same plant sale. Perhaps Tina Dodge introduced us, I have no recollection. But I'll never forget the result of however we heard about each other. Vividly, I recall the day Guy backed his dusty pickup up to Logee's Greenhouses (where I was working at the time) with a load of freshly thrown terracotta. Before that juncture, I had seen and dragged home plenty of nineteenth-century flowerpots from Britain. But this was my first encounter with the contemporary version being delivered to the door by the real live potter. It was a transformational moment. From then on, I could showcase plants in the manner they deserved.

That's my first memory of Guy—complete with red bandana, worn dunga-rees, and hysterical laugh. It's a wild laugh, a contagious laugh, a laugh like I've never heard before—the only possible analogy would be in the film *Amadeus*, but the film version in no way captures Guy's declaration of sheer glee. He was definitely not just another vendor; we became immediate friends. I was infinitely excited about the pots, to be sure. But I was also transfixed by his honesty and grounded simplicity. For example, Guy's signature packing material is straw—and I thought that was a brilliant, ecologically creative solution to the transportation problem. Turned out, the straw was quintessentially Guy. Practical, resourceful, simple, every inch Yankee but with flair and showmanship, Guy put a spin on pottery like nobody before or since.

My brother-in-law said that we'd never sell those pots, and he was right. Within a very short amount of time, I'd found an excuse to transplant every-thing from pelargoniums to clerodendrums into Guy Wolff pots until my entire inventory of hand-thrown terracotta had walked away from the sales area and was making our stock plants infinitely happy. Who could bear to part with those plants? Prouder and stronger due to their underpinnings, compared to their compatriots all around, those plants were keepers.

Of course, I wasn't the only one to discover Guy Wolff, as the pages of this book attest. So I don't think that I exaggerate when I say that Guy's impact on the horticultural scene was seismic. To give you a feeling for the atmosphere at the time, it was an era in which plant purveyors were flocking to embrace plastic, and clay was moving rapidly into obscurity. That migration could have spelled doom.

Given the leprechaun-green packaging that epitomized plastic flowerpots, potted plants lacked any sort of come-hither quality whatsoever to lure people to invite nature into their lives. The resulting product looked shabby. If Guy Wolff hadn't come along, we might have waved farewell to ornamental potted plants entirely.

This book does a very thorough job of covering the specifics of how Guy learned his craft. But what it doesn't talk about is how we found our way to Guy Wolff. After all, we're talking about flowerpots here—not your typical crowd pleasers that put artists in the public eye. Guy might have been the greatest potter known to mankind, but he would still be working in obscurity if it weren't for his passion. His enthusiasm sold his product. Make no mistake about it, we found Guy because of the fire in his belly. Guy Wolff makes a gorgeous flowerpot, it's true. But it is his overflowing, larger-than-life enthusiasm for his craft that really brought him into the limelight. It's all distilled into that laugh.

Then again, Guy could be the most flamboyant fellow in the universe, and he would be whistling in the dark if his product wasn't true. Beyond the fact that plants look like a million contained in Guy's creations, they are also happier. Argue with me if you will, but I cannot be convinced otherwise. Plastic is just not what root systems want. Roots revel in clay. Not only do they love the medium, but they delight in a custom fit—although he's not a gardener, heaven knows, Guy was sensitive enough to those who play in the dirt to ask for feedback and respond. When rosemary roots are given a pot where they can plummet straight down, and begonias are anchored in a container where their roots can stretch out, they thrive. They achieve their destiny.

After Guy blazed the path, plenty of potteries realized that there is an eager market for terracotta. At present, there are quantities of containers with the necessary dimensions to accommodate root systems comfortably. But not many pots have the singular beauty of Wolff's masterpieces. Thanks to his dedication, inventiveness, and pursuit of tradition, he found a way to produce a truly glorious product that thrills the soul. Horticulture as a whole has been the beneficiary. As a result of Guy's passion, plants everywhere are proudly sending their roots down (or out) and growing salubriously. When I think of Guy Wolff, my mind doesn't go straight to all the grand estates where his work dwells. Instead, I think of all the grateful begonias. And I think of all the people who have adopted those begonias to brighten their lives.

Tovah Martin HORTICULTURALIST, AUTHOR, PHOTO STYLIST
ROXBURY, CONNECTICUT

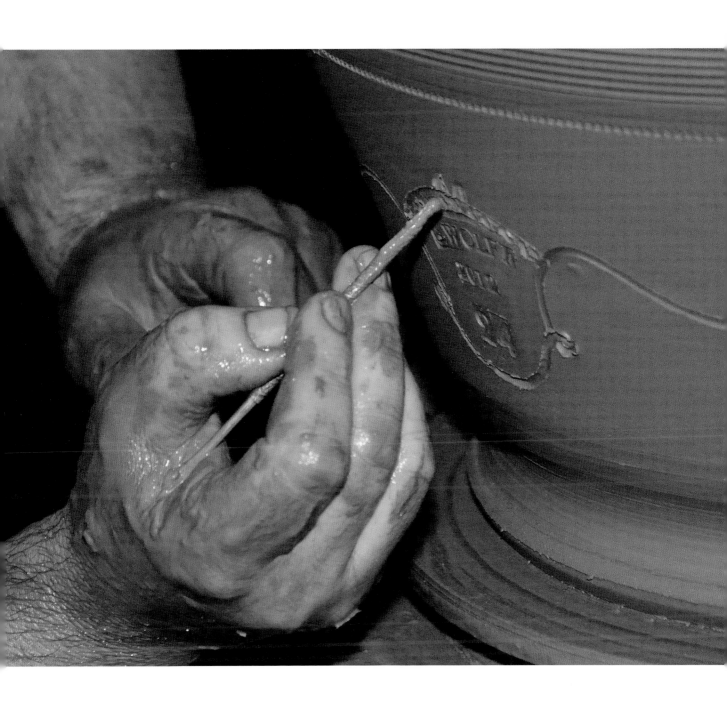

A charming hand-painted sign greets passersby and welcomes
everyone to Guy Wolff's pottery workshop in the postcard-pretty
Litchfield hills of Bantam, Connecticut.

Introduction

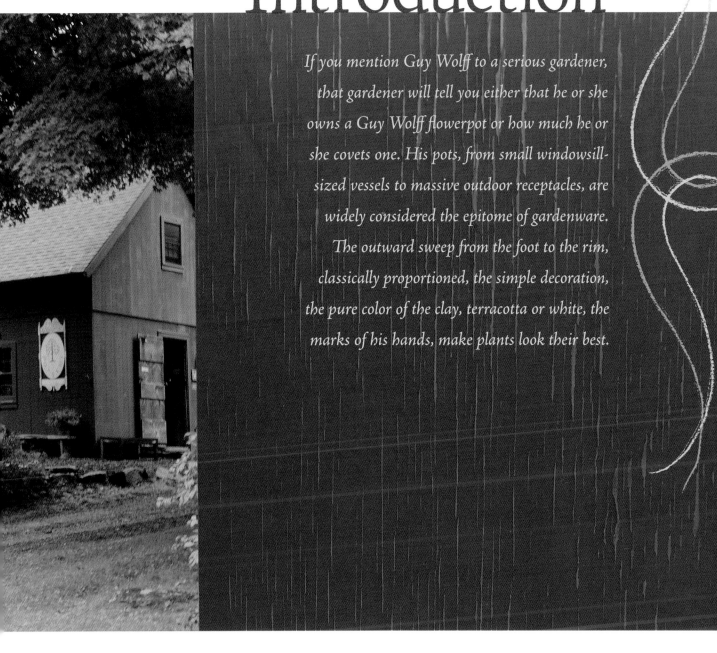

If you mention Guy Wolff to a serious gardener, that gardener will tell you either that he or she owns a Guy Wolff flowerpot or how much he or she covets one. His pots, from small windowsill-sized vessels to massive outdoor receptacles, are widely considered the epitome of gardenware.

The outward sweep from the foot to the rim, classically proportioned, the simple decoration, the pure color of the clay, terracotta or white, the marks of his hands, make plants look their best.

His pots possess an honesty and liveliness that machine-made flowerpots lack. They are beautiful and eminently functional, with generous drainage holes, a porous composition, and a shape that guarantees that a root ball can be slipped out for repotting when the time comes.

Wolff is probably the best-known potter working in the U.S. today. In gardening circles, he is highly revered, a horticultural icon. Gardeners flock to his lectures and demonstrations. Visit the personal gardens of landscape designers, and you will see Guy Wolff pots. Step inside the gates of estate gardens, and you will see Guy Wolff pots.

Ironically, his pots have been on the cover of *Horticulture Magazine*, but not on the cover of *Ceramics Monthly* (the potters' magazine of record). Yet he is a potter's potter. He's a big ware thrower, a skill few have today. He thinks deeply about what he calls the architecture of pots and the importance of handmade objects in our lives. He learned from some of the best traditional potters in Wales and England, disciplining himself to be able to throw a half-ton of clay a day, as the old-time throwers did. He has steeped himself in the history of ceramics, especially the ceramics of Italy, France, England, Wales, and early America. He supports himself, sometimes tenuously, with what he makes. And he has succeeded in reaching an interesting accommodation with the realities of the modern marketplace and has established guilds of potters.

The day I first met with him for this book, he was carrying an 80-pound pot from his drying boards to one of his kilns for ten hours of candling at 200°F. This lengthy period of low heat would ensure that all the water would be removed from the large garden vessel (taller than my youngest granddaughter) so that it could be safely fired. Entering his seventh decade, a red bandanna tied tightly on his head, with thick arms, a slight belly in the way of a man who has lived a certain number of years, average height, an air of seriousness and purpose, he measures his days in making time.

He says he has been very lucky. More than once, he says, things have all just come together and happened for him. But he has had his share of challenges too, and worked to face and overcome them.

Wolff first set up shop in Woodville, a small hamlet in the postcard-pretty northwestern hills of Connecticut in 1971. Today his shop is in a small eighteenth-century two-room house that he expanded. The front, the original house, is his showroom, lined with shelves displaying his flowerpots and other pieces. Across the back of the house, in an addition, is his workspace, crowded with three wheels, three kilns, a pugmill and ware boards. His treasured coggles, the carved caster-like wheels he uses for decorating, hang along the wall, objets d'art themselves. There is a loft over the showroom. Here he keeps his wonderful collection of the pots that he admires and takes inspiration from, and, close to the floor, under the eaves, shelves of gardening and ceramics books. Up the hill from the shop and behind it are his wife Erica's abundant gardens punctuated with Wolff's pots, which she has planted, and the handmade house they share. North of the workshop is an outbuilding with special racks for his father's paintings. Except for these wrapped and racked abstract expressionist paintings by his famous father, Robert Jay Wolff, the bucolic setting is exactly what you would imagine for a country potter working either today or one hundred years ago. It is also the home and workshop of the cosmopolitan artist-potter, businessman-potter that he is; one who travels to China and Honduras to work with the Guilds, who rubs shoulders with celebrity, who gives talks and demonstrations all over the country, whose name is a household word to gardeners, and whose work is collected by connoisseurs.

A gardener and potter myself, I very much admire Wolff's pottery and take pleasure in looking at his life and his art in these pages. His is an unusual story that I think will interest not only potters and gardeners but anyone curious about how a person in the twenty-first century can move in a direction opposite to that of the cultural tide that has been sweeping our society since the mid-twentieth century, and live by the hand.

Wolff is deeply committed to his family. Blessed with three sons, a daughter, and a talented wife who is the yin to his yang, he says, "They are the reason I work so hard." In these pages, however, we will focus on his life in clay.

The book is based on multiple lengthy interviews with Wolff and with those who know him or have interacted with him. He has a pre-Aristotelian mind, belonging almost more to an oral tradition than a written one, keeping vast stores of names, events, pot shapes, and other information in his mind. He has a truly prodigious memory and a knack for storytelling. His speech is colorful, running forward, stopping in mid-sentence, racing ahead, and then doubling back, and he is often throwing pot after pot as he talks. I have tried to capture his voice on the page, quoting him extensively, but a sentence spoken is not the same as a sentence written. I hope I have succeeded in bringing him and his pots to you here, between these covers. But I suggest, if you can, after you have come to know him here, you go and visit him in his small workshop in Bantam, Connecticut, watch him work, listen to a story, and then treat yourself to one of his very beautiful pots.

Wolff removes a majestic, freshly thrown
flowerpot from his wheel.

CHAPTER ONE

Guy Wolff

MASTER POTTER

Wolff says it's "the bones of a pot that matter."
When he looks at a piece he likes, most often
vintage country pottery, he says he is "interested in
the architectural decisions the potter made to get
the clay to move." He tries to visualize how "to get
from point A to point B in the least moves." It is his
notion of the least moves that is one of the defining
principles of his work, and what gives his pots their
energy. This is counterintuitive. We think of modern
craftspeople as taking their time, of handwork by
definition being slow work. But pottery, Wolff
believes, is different. He is not alone in this.

"Unlike other mass-produced art, hand-thrown pots seem to look better the faster they are turned out," John Windsor wrote for the Sunday *Independent* in 1995. "The potter's skill improves with practice—yet there is no time for pretentiousness. Hence the charm of English country pottery made for cooking, baking, brewing, storing, growing seedlings, or feeding chickens."[1]

Windsor was writing about a collection of early English country pottery that had recently come onto the market and explaining to his urban readers why these simple pots from the past resonated with modern cooks. These are the pots that Wolff admires. A measure of his achievement is that Windsor's words could equally describe the appeal of Wolff's wares. Quickly and robustly thrown, in multiples, his pots, like the old-time pots, touch us.

Among the offerings at that auction were a few pots made by one of Wolff's personal heroes, Isaac Button, the "last true English country potter." Wolff says he loves to watch the black-and-white video that the photographer/filmmaker John Anderson made of Button in 1965, four years before Button's death at 66. "It's one of my favorites," Wolff smiles. "It's a window into the last breath of preindustrial pottery."

Button worked at Soil Hill, which had been a pottery since 1780 when Jonathan Catherall set it up. By 1884, Button's grandfather was there, and later his father. At one time thirteen potters made wares to fill the big coal-fired kiln, but in the last decades Button worked alone, doing everything himself. He dug and processed the clays, mixed slip, threw, glazed, and fired alone. It was hard physical work. He made cider jars, horticultural wares, jugs, cups, milk pans and other items for the farm and kitchen. In the film, which Wolff never tires of watching, you see him with a bib apron tied on over his jacket, a pipe in his mouth, a cravat at his neck, as he deftly throws cup after cup, seemingly without effort. Making a tall jar, he smiles to himself when it is done. "In a day," Windsor wrote, "he could turn a ton of clay into pots. I timed him as he threw a lump of clay on to the wheel, pulled it high, then cut it off with wire: 22 seconds. In an hour, he could turn out 120 pots. In a day, 1,200."[2]

Wolff is working in a different era but his skills at the wheel rival Button's. "When you are working in any medium you have to understand the attributes of the material and understand what it is meant to do," he says. "You have to have a reverence for the material." With clay, he explains, "it is motion and compression, just as with music it is sound and silence, or photography: light and dark."

Wolff's wheels are electric, high-end Shimpo Whispers made in Japan. When throwing, he runs his wheel at a fast speed and has both the wheel and his seat elevated, much like a kick wheel. He has built himself a simple wooden stool, not to sit on but to lean against. For big pots, he stands on cement blocks so that he can work over the wheelhead and reach his arm all the way down into the bottom interior of the pot.

Wolff can easily throw fifty pounds of clay into a tall arm's-length jar. Certainly he is not the only potter with this skill, but he does it with extraordinary ease. Most potters cannot handle such a large mass, or must work by adding coils rather than throwing straight up.

He begins by throwing a twelve-pound ball of clay onto the wheel. He centers this and then throws another ball onto it, and centers the two together, followed by a third. Centering is how all pots begin on the wheel. The potter exerts pressure on the spinning clay until it is a smooth, perfectly symmetrical cone.

After centering, for large pots, he uses the heel of his left hand on the outside of the pot for his first pull. After that, or for smaller wares, he uses his right knuckle on the exterior, four inches below his left hand on the interior. In this way he is able to pull a lot of clay up to great heights.

He throws with extraordinary speed. Watching him, you can see that he is pulling a lot of clay. It bulges over his knuckle, so much that the pot wobbles just a bit and looks almost as if it might collapse. But it does not. And at a stage where most potters would stop pulling and thinning, he pulls once more, the wheel still at high speed. For most of his pots, he leaves a thick rim at the top and if you are an experienced thrower yourself, you might wonder why the weight of that thick rim is not creating a ruinous torque in the thin walls or tearing them. Then he takes his rib and within seconds the clay is compressed, the pot perfectly true to center. At this stage he uses almost no water. With the rib he makes the final shape and then what he calls the "fun" begins: he makes the rim and adds a bit of decoration.

"Materials have intent," he says. "Manipulating is a dead end. Dancing is what makes for conversation." Indeed, his throwing is a fast waltz with the clay, magical to watch. "The best old pots are very serious conversations," he continues, once again expressing his deep appreciation for time-honored ways at the wheel.

"When you are making a pot, certain things have to happen. There are architectural decisions that have to be made. Pots have arches, domes and straights. If you are making a traditional English flowerpot, the fastest way to get from point A to point B is with an arch. So the first and second move might be just getting the clay up from the bottom to the top in this very fast arch and then in the last moment the clay is domed out where it is not arched, so what you get is a Dorian line: arch, dome, arch, that you see in millions of flower pots. One might go, 'So, you want to copy that shape?' No, I want to copy the *reason* why that shape is so strong. I want to make a decision about it. Guys who were making really nice jugs one day were making tonnage of horticultural pots another. They made architectural decisions on how to get the clay to move to the desired shape." He adds that he has spent his life "trying to understand what made the pots that drew" him "so good. So over and over again, for decades, it's been a visual exercise in understanding how you get from point A to point B with the least amount of moves."

Wolff says that new potters are usually better at movement than at compression. Yet, he says he sees many potters throwing with a sponge or using their fingertips to throw, "not the way to move a lot of clay." They are left with thick bases, which require trimming, and, because less clay is moved, the pots are shorter.

LEFT
Using his forearm,
Wolff centers the first
12-pound ball of clay
for a 24-pound pot.

RIGHT
Centering the second
ball of clay on top
of the first for a total
of 24 pounds.

LEFT
Wolff opens the pot.

BELOW
Pulling the clay up.
Using his knuckle on
the outside, Wolff
moves a lot of clay.

For compression and for shaping the pot, he uses a rib on the exterior. It is a large metal rib, straight, with a wooden top for grasping. "The rib is to the potter the same thing as the violin bow is to the fiddle," he says. "A rib has a wider stance than a finger. You can compress more clay with a rib." He returns to the concept of arches, straights, and domes and says that the three basic moves for them are very formalized. "If you hold the rib in towards your belly, at a 45-degree angle, that makes arches; if you hold the rib straight up and down, with the pivot in the middle, that makes a straight, and if you hold it at a 45-degree angle away from your belly, and the top is towards your chin, you get a dome. How you hold your interior hand, adds the subtext . . . There are laws behind every form that you come upon." Wolff has spent years thinking about these laws, absorbing them with his hands and body as much as with his

LEFT
Wolff continues to
pull and move the clay
up as the wheel spins.

CENTER
Wolff keeps the rim
thicker than the rest
of the pot for later
decoration with
a coggle.

RIGHT
Wolff shapes the rim.

BOTTOM
Wolff compresses
the clay with a rib,
smoothing the outer
walls as the rib rises
from the base to the
rim of the pot.

mind. Yet watching him throw, it looks intuitive. There is a relaxed ease to his movements. And looking at his pieces, what you see is the vigor of the forms, not the laws that guided them.

Wolff holds a large metal rib in his right hand. "This is Frank Parsley's rib," he says with a hint of a sparkle in his eyes. You know a story is coming. Wolff loves to tell a story, and is comfortable talking while he works, chatting with visitors to his shop, talking while he demonstrates at gardening seminars.

When he was in his early twenties and his shop had only been open for a year and a half, he was approached by the Disney studios to make a large quantity of salt-glazed works. He decided to visit Brannam Pottery in Barnstaple in Devon, England, to see how a large pottery managed big orders.

After learning all the skills necessary to make good pots, Thomas Brannam founded Brannam Pottery in 1847 in the English pottery village of Barnstaple. He made tiles,

LEFT
Wolff coggles
the top of the rim.

BELOW
Wolff stamps the pot
with his name and the
weight, 24 pounds.

sewer pipes, and domestic ware. His son Charles Hubert Brannam joined him, eventually inheriting the business. He changed the direction of the firm and began making art pottery. Queen Victoria placed an order and suddenly Brannam Pottery was famous. As was the custom, Charles added "royal" to the name, and called their work Royal Brannam Ware. After his death in 1937, the pottery returned to rustic, domestic pottery.

When Wolff visited, Frank Parsley was the big ware potter. He was producing pots for the Queen Mother, including large horticultural ware. At that time, studio pottery was much sought after, but interest in old-style country pottery had declined. Parsley was 62 and eager to pass on his skills, but he had not found an apprentice to whom to pass them. He invited Wolff to apprentice and agreed to stay on for four more years to work with him if he accepted.

Wolff was excited by the opportunity and rushed to find a phone and call home to tell his family of his new plans. His mother answered, and quietly told him that his father had been stricken with a severe heart attack. Wolff walked back to Brannam's and told Parsley that he could not take the apprenticeship after all, and would instead be returning to the U.S., to his mother and ailing father.

Disappointed but understanding, Parsley gave Wolff two ribs as a parting gift and token of encouragement. Wolff treasured them. With use, especially the constant use of what Wolff calls a tonnage thrower like himself, ribs wear out. But he liked using Parsley's ribs so much, the way they felt in his hand, the work they did on the walls of his pots, that he had a local metal shop reproduce them, a practice he continues to this day. He also uses discarded bread dough scrapers from a local bakery as ribs. As with his pots, Wolff is reinterpreting a tradition by repurposing bread dough scrapers. Indeed, John Anderson writes in *Making Pottery*, Wolff's potter hero Button cut his ribs from old spades.[3]

Wolff's horticultural wares are made of either red or white earthenware. He says that throwing with earthenware is "like a date with a very easygoing person who likes to go dancing. It is," he explains, "wetter, more oily, more languid," than stoneware. In contrast, throwing stoneware is "like having tea with your grandmother."

He cuts and lifts most of his pots directly from the wheelhead and sets them onto a ware board to dry. Except for the largest pieces, he prefers to work without bats (discs made of wood, plaster, or plastic that potters fasten to their wheelheads, so they can lift the bat rather than the pot itself, making it easy to remove a pot without distorting it). He does, however, have a trick for lifting large pots without distorting them, which he learned from the potters at "a great old pottery near Porto" in Portugal. He had been brought in to help them re-find their direction in their own pot making. While there, he saw that the old potters had fashioned round, hinged circles of wood that they placed inside their larger pots so that they would not distort when they were lifted off the wheel. No need for bats. "I use more than one [stacked one atop the other like pancakes] as the pots get bigger. A twenty-pounder comes off the wheel like a two-pounder."

Until he was 56, Wolff mixed his own clay. Then, suffering from mild silicosis, he began having it mixed for him at ceramic supply houses. In the first years of his shop, he used a Devonshire bonding clay called Vit-Red and added AP Green Fireclay, M&D Ball clay and up to 8 percent sand of various sizes. As his pots became larger, he increased the fireclay. He turned to Redart for his flowerpots, again adding fireclay and sand, more for larger pieces.

Wolff may slightly fettle the outside edge of the base of a pot, but, proudly, he does not trim. To fire without cracking or warping, walls must be of an even

Freshly thrown flowerpots, set upside down on ware boards, air drying in the workshop.

thickness, especially in large pots, so if the base of the wall is thicker than the upper portion, the pot must be partially dried and then set back on the wheel-head upside down and trimmed with a trimming tool while it spins. Wolff abhors the idea of "cutting partially dry clay." Because he pulls so much material up from the base when he throws, he does not need to trim. His walls are of an even thickness, except when he deliberately leaves a thickness at the rim to coggle. Similarly, he does not need or desire to trim the base or cut foot rings into them. He might run his hands across the base to smooth it a bit, and then he signs his name in the damp clay using his small finger as a writing instrument. He makes his drainage holes while he is throwing and the pot is wet.

Eighteenth- and nineteenth-century potters in the U.K. and America stamped their pots with numbers that related to the cast (unit) of clay that was used. Horticultural ware was standardized by size and weight, and always referenced the cast number. Potters were paid by how much clay they threw (we would call it piecework today), so it was important to them to stamp a pot's number so the weights could be totaled at the end of the workday. Pots were also priced for sale using the cast number. Similarly, Wolff stamps his pots and prices accordingly, though his numbers refer directly to the weight in pounds used for each pot and not the English cast number. For instance, his #6 English Full Pot is 9 inches tall by 9.25 inches wide at the rim and is made from six pounds of clay. As with the old-time potters, he stamps the number on the front of the pot, midway between the rim and foot along with his name and the date. The number is part of the decoration.

An ever-growing assortment of coggles and roulettes hangs on Wolff's wall, close to his wheel. A coggle is a little wheel with a handle, similar to a caster or pizza cutter, which is used to impress a repeating design around a pot. They were widely employed by seventeenth- and eighteenth-century British slipware potters. He has coggles for two-dimensional and three-dimensional designs. He makes them from found objects or carves them from clay, which he fires before using. "One of my most useful coggles," he says, "I made from the lid of a peanut butter jar!" It makes a nice band of little lines. He can spend as much as ten hours sculpting a rope coggle, "but it's worth it when you see how they come out."

Wolff has metal strips fabricated for text. He nails each lettered strip to a wooden wheel, adds a handle, and has a coggle for quickly adding words, usually names, to his pots. He uses one to sign the bottoms of his pots in addition to his handwritten signature. When he has an order for pots made specifically for

Detail of coggled rim. Wolff has strips of metal fabricated with the lettering "G. Wolff Bantam, CT." or the name of the botanical garden or estate ordering his pots, then affixes the strip to a coggle wheel that he has made.

a particular place, such as The Brooklyn Botanical Garden, he makes a coggle with the place name just for those pots.

Since 1989 or 1990, he is not quite sure, Wolff has fired primarily in electric kilns. The expense of gas plus environmental concerns led to his decision to switch from fuel to electricity, and he now fires in three large, octagonal Skutts. "Electricity," he says, "is a lot more green than propane."

He begins a fire around 5:30 in the afternoon, with the top of the kiln open, keeping the temperature below 200°F. Around 9:30 p.m. he closes the top and lets the temperature climb to 2,000°F, making the pots strong enough to withstand frost, but not ice-proof. By the following evening, he can unstack. If he is firing a large piece, such as one of his eighty-pound full pots, he can fire only one at a time. Smaller pots can be stacked close together in the kiln and fired in quantity.

Wolff devotes most of his time to his horticultural wares. Right after Christmas, he begins throwing and firing wholesale flowerpot orders. He takes one week off in February to work with Mrs. Karl, his first pottery teacher, for a May Day sale. Around April 15, he starts throwing horticultural pots for retail, selling through his shop and various events, primarily large garden and flower shows. In July, he makes glazed jugs, tall jars, milk pans, bowls and such for the holidays.

Recently, he has rediscovered his early fascination with English slipwares and, taking a brief break from flowerpots, he makes joggled plates and huge,

Handsome slip-trailed
and joggled plates for sale
in Wolff's eighteenth-
century showroom.

Slip-trailed plates.
The large center plate
with the green apple
tree is 28 inches in
diameter.

slip-decorated chargers. For the joggled ware, he rolls out wet clay for slabs to make plates. While wet, he washes them with colored slip and then slip trails on top of the wet clay, making it possible to "joggle the colored slips and make swirling designs that look much like marbled end pages in Victorian books. After the round slab has hardened a few hours, it is draped over a hump mold and finished." He might use white slip as a base over the earthenware, and a contrasting white slip with 5 percent copper for a contrasting green. He throws the chargers, some approaching thirty pounds, and slip trails crosshatches, trees, names: his interpretations of traditional designs.

Wolff makes a lot of pots. Literally tons. He smiles, "One of the great phrases in the pottery world is 'the first thousand are the hardest.' In other words it takes a thousand to learn to make a shape." Indeed, he makes many thousands of each of his beautiful shapes.

Wolff's pot, in use for many years in the garden, has come to look
as antique as the old wheelbarrow that serves as its pedestal.

CHAPTER TWO

Flowerpots through the Millennia

Wolff is widely respected as a leading authority on the history of flowerpots, particularly those made in the eighteenth and nineteenth centuries. He needs little persuasion to share his capacious knowledge of ceramic history or admiration for his potter-hero antecedents. His enthusiasm is infectious.

"It really doesn't matter if someone owns Campbell Soup [Company] or has three pots in the backyard," Wolff says. "You start putting dirt into a flowerpot and people are changed because they are doing something that is nurturing. When a person sees a mother with a newborn or even a toddler and the kid looks at your face and smiles, you could be Adolf Eichmann and you'd still be [touched] and it's the same thing with gardening. People who might have a crazy life otherwise are completely transfixed when they are dealing with the magic of a plant in a pot."

When the College of the Atlantic on Mount Desert Island, Maine, asked the garden historian Susan Tamulevich to create a new exhibit to succeed her successful exhibit about Dumbarton Oaks, she thought of her encounters with Wolff over the years and suggested a show on flowerpots. The College agreed and she created the popular traveling exhibit "A Place to Take Root: The History of Flowerpots and Garden Containers in North America."

"Guy was the inspiration," she says, "he provided examples of regional American pots; and Jim Keeling of Whichford Pottery provided examples of traditional British horticultural ware. Other potters contributed contemporary and historic designs."

"A Place to Take Root" has been shown throughout the United States and generated stories in the *Washington Post, New York Times, Christian Science Monitor,* and elsewhere. The exhibit, which includes antique pots, horticultural pots made by Wolff and Keeling, and often a demonstration by Wolff at the openings, has given American gardeners a greater appreciation for flowerpots.

Gardeners have been growing plants in pots for thousands of years. Anyone who has seen little shoots sprout out of his or her garlic before having a chance to cook with it understands how obvious an idea a garden pot is. Instantly, the garlic pot in the cupboard is transformed into a plant pot. Perhaps a Neolithic housewife, instead of tossing the sprout onto the waste heap or feeding it to the livestock, thought it was pretty and kept it. From this happenstance, it was not much of a leap to purposely plant in a vessel, thus making plants portable. "Pots," Wolff says, "move with plants."

We know from tomb paintings that ancient Egyptians were accomplished gardeners. The wealthy built arbors, understood irrigation, and created beautiful outdoor enclosures. They loved symmetry and were early proponents of what we would call formal gardening. For emphasis, they placed planted pots atop their garden walls and at key points within the garden itself. [1]

Egyptian potters mastered the wheel and threw beautifully. They built small beehive-shaped kilns similar to their bread ovens and were able to control their firing process. Interestingly, the pots in the tomb paintings are startlingly similar to some of Wolff's pots: practical, with wide mouths and flat bases. He does not claim the ancient Egyptian horticultural ware as his inspiration, but potters have been sharing, copying, and passing down information for thousands of years. There is perhaps an unconscious, collective memory.

Egyptian royalty enjoyed collecting plants from distant lands and built large pleasure gardens to show off their imported trees. Queen Hatshepsut (1495–1475 BCE) sent an expedition in two ships to trade goods with the king and inhabitants of the mysterious land of Punt. The ships returned with panthers, monkeys, gold, precious stones, and 31 incense trees that had been dug up with their roots intact and transported in baskets and large flowerpots. All but one of the trees survived the journey and Hatshepsut had them planted in her palace garden. There are pictures and an account of the expedition in her tomb.

Three and a half centuries later, Ramses III (1198–1166 BCE) indulged his horticultural love affair by building 514 semi-public temple gardens, accented with pots. Despite their arid climate, ancient Egyptians grew vegetables, fruits, herbs, trees, and flowers. They favored greenery or perhaps herbs over colorful flowers in their pots, though it appears they did grow some flowers.

This formal style of garden prevailed throughout the Near and Middle East and later blossomed into the fabulous paradisiacal gardens of Islam. Magnificent gardens were made in India and Pakistan, Turkey, Syria, Egypt, Spain, Sicily, Morocco, and Algeria. Symmetrical, enclosed, and formal, they reflected earth, air, fire and water. Flowerpots were carefully placed at the intersections of paths.

Early Greek society emphasized the public sphere over the private. Homes were not equipped with gardens until Epicurus (c. 250 BCE) built one for his house (according to Pliny the Elder).[2] Agriculture took place outside the city limits, away from discourse and trade. Archeologists have found flowerpots in the courtyards of some houses, however, suggesting families did grow potted plants at home even though they eschewed gardens.

Flowerpots were also crucial to the cult of Adonis that was popular with the women of Greece and later Rome. To honor the death of Adonis, and metaphorically the changing seasons, seeds would be planted in pots (often broken pots). Once the seeds had sprouted, the pot was carried up to the roof and the plants left to wither and die.

Greek potters preserved a wealth of information about Greek life by painting images in slip on their wares. One extant vase, now in the Karlsruhe Museum in Germany, shows Venus on a ladder. Her son, the winged Cupid, is handing her a flared flowerpot of sprouts. At Cupid's feet are two more garden pots, one a pedestal shape. Both are also planted. It appears that Venus is going to bring all three pots up to her rooftop.

The Adonis cult and attendant roof pots were even more popular in ancient Rome. Romans, however, were so taken with the looks of flowers, elaborate topiaries, and greenery growing in pots that in addition to the Adonis pots, they set planted pots in their windows, on their rooftops, under the eaves of the colonnades of their homes, and in the gardens and courtyards attached to their houses. Lower-class Romans, who could not afford grand homes and lived in apartment buildings, kept flowerpots on their windowsills and carefully tended them. Pliny the Elder lamented the need for window bars to keep out thieves in such areas and complained that the bars blocked the view of the window gardens from passersby in the street below.[3]

Often, flowerpots were the Roman's version of recycling. Rather than toss a broken amphorae or cooking pot, they would plant a few seeds in it. But they also had purposely made flowerpots. Cato gives directions for three different ways to use a flowerpot to propagate trees and shrubs.[4]

Romans built villas, baths, and gardens throughout their vast empire, thus spreading their ideas about decoration and horticulture. They constructed brickworks and pot shops and shared (or imposed) their potter's wheels, molds, and kilns upon distant lands.

After the Empire crumbled and the Dark Ages ensued, much knowledge was lost. The Roman baths in the northern reaches of the Empire in what is now England fell into disrepair. The grand villas with their rows of potted plants were vandalized and left in ruins. Domestic pottery was still produced, but it was less refined.

The marriage of pottery and horticulture also thrived in China. The Chinese built enormous kilns and mastered the arts of stoneware and porcelain, firing for days and consuming whole forests until they reached the high temperatures necessary for these clays to mature. They loved a curve more than a straight line and made gardens with winding paths rather than the geometric beds favored around the Mediterranean. They placed their flowerpots so that they would be a pleasant surprise for strollers coming around the bend. Chinese potters also made fishponds, garden seats, and vases.

China consolidated and split apart repeatedly for thousands of years, but ceramics was important to each of the eras. Today, we associate particular styles with the different dynasties: simple, subtly glazed pots of the Sung, where form prevailed over decoration; the bright multicolored glazes of the Tang; the enamels and blues and whites of the later years. They loved flowers, especially the chrysanthemum and the peony, and carved or painted them on their vases and bowls and flowerpots. A pot could have a flower within and without.

Chinese ceramics influenced the potter's art in much of the world. Their fine blue and white porcelain was prized and imitated for many years in the Near and Middle East and in Europe before the secret of its manufacture was discovered. Some authorities see Sung influence in the traditional alkaline glazed pots of the American South.

Until the Chinese learned to fire their kilns to high temperatures, all pottery was low-fired. The Romans called it *terra cotta* (baked earth). Flowerpots continued to be low-fired as the porosity of earthenware suits plants best, although porcelain and stoneware have been used for decorative purposes.

As Europe emerged from the Dark Ages into the Middle Ages and the Renaissance, horticulture was reborn and with it a rekindled interest in formal garden design. The Florentine Luca della Robbia (c. 1400–1482 CE) set up shop and began making terracotta garden ornaments, including lifesize statuary, plaques, and pots decorated with sprigs and swags. His work was in great demand.

Large pots were needed for the newly popular potted citrus trees. Wealthy gardeners built orangeries to overwinter these trees, often heating them with heaps of steaming manure. Potters made the necessarily enormous pots by coiling thick rolls of clay in molds. Plant hunters traveled the globe in pursuit of new plants and shipped their finds home to their patrons or for their own experimental gardens. Nurserymen began cultivating and selling plants in vast quantities. The demand for flowerpots was insatiable. Potters saw the market for their kitchenwares diminish with the advent of trains and the movement of food and goods across long distances. A housewife did not need to purchase an earthen crock from a local potter if she was no longer churning her own cream into butter but instead buying industrially produced butter that was transported from a commercial buttery a great distance away into town by rail. Happily, potters were kept busy supplying nurserymen with millions of pots. With the invention of plate glass in 1833, greenhouses became more practical, and soon plants came indoors as decoration. Demand for flowerpots remained high.

English potters standardized their wares by weight and shape. They threw plain pots and fancy rimmed pots; what they called "full pots" in many sizes;

Rubens Peale with Geranium by Rembrandt Peale,
the painting that gave Wolff some of his most important
inspiration. Wolff keeps a copy of the painting on the wall
of his shop. Courtesy of the National Gallery

shorter and squatter "half pots"; and tall, narrow long toms. They rolled and pounded out slabs to make square and rectangular seedpans, a more laborious process than throwing, but favored by the nurserymen as they economized on space.

The Industrial Revolution brought mechanization to pottery making. The jigger and jolley were invented, speeding up the production of pots. Fewer and less skilled potters were required to work in these great urban factories that came to dominate the craft. Entire families worked in the Stoke-on-Trent potteries, even the children. Smoke from the kilns darkened the city skies. In the U.S., flowerpots were almost entirely factory-made by the end of the Civil War.

In rural settings in England, country potters continued to work for another century, but then they too succumbed to the competition of factory-made pots. In the early 1960s, nurseries switched to the plastic pots we see today. A decade later, American studio potters were making hanging pots strung with macramé, but the traditional hand-thrown flowerpot was nearly extinct.

Wolff makes a flowerpot he calls the Peale Pot. It has a thickened rim, and immediately below the rim, a second decorative ropelike band. He says he was "inspired by the portrait of Rubens Peale, 1801 Philadelphia." The portrait, painted by Rembrandt Peale (1778–1860) of his younger, horticulturally minded brother, shows the young man with a flowerpot planted with a red pelargonium. Seeing the painting was an epiphany for Wolff.

Pelargoniums are native to the Cape of South Africa where they thrive in the hot, dry climate. The great plant explorer John Tradescant (1570–1638) is often associated with the pelargonium and indeed the first record of a pelargonium growing in England was in John Gerard's (1545–1612) *Herball* (1633) in which he describes one growing in Tradescant's south London garden. Tradescant noted that he received six geraniums, "Reseved in the yeare 1631 from Mr. Rene Morin . . . Geranium noctu odoratu." Anne Wilkinson speculates in *The Passion for Pelargoniums* that Morin, a Frenchman who with his brother specialized in bulbs, got his plants in Holland as the Dutch were engaged in trade with the West Indies by way of the Cape.[5] In 1609, H. Peter Loewer tells us in *Jefferson's Garden*, the governor of the Cape had sent some geraniums to Holland with a shipment of bulbs and by 1710 sailors were bringing them back to Europe for their wives and girlfriends. Morin gave or sold some to Tradescant.[6]

Jefferson grew geraniums both in the White House and, upon his retirement in 1809, at Monticello. He may have sent some back to himself during one of his visits to France. Or he or someone else may have sent one to Rembrandt Peale's father, Charles Wilson Peale (1741–1827), who was a correspondent of Jefferson's. An artist himself, Charles Wilson Peale painted Jefferson's portrait. He also ran a museum in Philadelphia. Rubens knew that Jefferson had the pelargonium on his plant list and, in the painting, looks pleased to have one himself. Wolff is intrigued that we don't know whether the pot in the painting was made in England or America, nor do we know whether Jefferson gave the geranium to Peale or Peale gave it to him. He suspects, however, that Peale gave Jefferson a cutting, and that descendants of that cutting grow at Monticello today, which he realizes is perhaps a romantic notion. The curator of plants at Monticello gave

Pot inspired by the 1801 painting, *Rubens Peale with Geranium,* by Rembrandt Peale. Like all his pots, Wolff makes the Peale, with its wonderfully coggled rim, in various sizes. This one is 4 pounds, thrown in 2011.

him a cutting from the Peale geranium, which he has grown into a full plant that overlooks his dining table.

When Rembrandt Peale painted the picture of his younger brother with a potted geranium, the flower was still a rarity in North America but it would soon become popular. "They were ubiquitous in the beginning of the nineteenth century," Susan Condor writes in *The Complete Geranium*, "and during the late Victorian period, when they were cultivated in their thousands by nurserymen and avid enthusiasts. Whole greenhouses were devoted exclusively to raising geraniums."[7] The geraniums in those greenhouses were grown in flowerpots.

Wolff first saw the Peale painting during the seventies while at the Massachusetts Horticultural Society. What excited him was that this Georgian-era pot (1714–1837) was for ornamental purposes. He fell in love with the braid of the double rim.

With his Peale Pot, Wolff references a well-known American painting and the horticultural history that lies behind it. He references the thousands of years we have been growing plants in pots and specifically references the horticultural ware of English and American country potters when they were doing their most robust works.

He says his work is "less about facts than about intent." His Peale Pot is not a reproduction of the pot in the painting but an expression of the essence of ornamental pots of that era.

Thus we see flowerpots have a long and interesting history, from the Neolithic stirrings of agriculture, through the ancient worlds of the Egyptians and Greeks and Romans, and reaching great heights during the era of botanic exploration and the florescence of the horticulture industry. During the Industrial Revolution, thrown pots were replaced by the factory-made terracotta pots that we are all familiar with, and these in turn were replaced, in the mid-twentieth century, with shiny green plastic pots. Wolff entered this history at a time when more pots than ever before were manufactured, but they were no longer objects in and of themselves. They were (and are) made without the touch of a human hand. Wolff has, from the beginning of his career, insisted on the necessity of that touch. He demands that his pots exude the energy of life itself.

CHAPTER THREE

Early Years
& Influences

*How do we become the people we become?
Why does one person take up carpentry
with a passion and another watercolors or
botany? Why did Guy Wolff, the son of a
well-connected abstract expressionist artist,
become a rural potter? Was it the family
artist-gene gone its own way? The result
of the external influences that swirled
around his childhood? The times?*

Social scientists and neuroscientists ask the same questions about each of us, but so far the answers elude them. In Wolff's case, it is probably all and none of these. By the time Wolff was born, his father, Robert Jay Wolff (1905–1977), had won prizes for his sculpture, was an important abstract expressionist artist, and was an intimate within a close circle of ground-breaking and well-known artists and architects.

"I was almost born at the [Alexander] Calder house," Wolff says of the close friendship between his parents and the Calders. "My mom was pregnant with me the summer of 1950. Sandy and Louisa went off to Provence for the summer and needed a family to stay near 'Granma Calder' (being in her 80s at the time). So my parents had a nice summer in the country staying at the Calder house . . . and I came along on September second, being born in the New Milford hospital."[1]

The Calder residence was an eighteenth-century farmhouse on Painter Hill Road in Roxbury, Connecticut. After living in France for years, the Calders returned to the U.S. in 1933 amid rumors of war and purchased the old run-down house and the eighteen acres that surrounded it, plus an icehouse and fire-damaged barn, for $3,500. They painted the exterior of the house black after a fire, a perfect foil for the outdoor sculptures (it is still the only black colonial in the Litchfield Hills), turned the icehouse into a studio, and filled the place with Calder's art.[2]

On Thanksgiving Day two years after Wolff was born, the Calder's younger daughter and Wolff's father found a house for the Wolff family in nearby Washington, Connecticut. Alas, Wolff says, to everyone's surprise, "It turned out the house was in the middle of the road!" The house hunters had neglected to walk the land and so they saw only that the house was set on a hill, facing a quiet country road. What they didn't notice was that, slicing close behind the house, almost parallel to the road in front of the house, was the new and improved Route 202, a busy state road. Nevertheless, his father built a studio there and the family moved in.

"My father was the son of a very wealthy guy, the first person to do wholesale drugs for American Pharmacy," Wolff says. "He went to Yale where his roommates were Andrew Goodman, Gardiner Stern, and M. Spiegel. He was supposed to run a store. He went to London to study about tweeds and tailoring, but he ran away to Paris to learn sculpture and painting. My father's father said that he 'gave up his job for his work.'"

After three years of college, Robert Jay Wolff dropped out and began a promising career in the men's clothing business at Hart, Schaffner and Marx, under the stewardship of his "foster uncle," Uncle Al Levy (Alexander M. Levy), a close friend of his father.[3] He did very well, contributed some highly original and commercially successful ideas, designed men's clothing and came up with a winning advertising campaign, but writing and drawing all the while; he left the safety of the firm, and, radically for his family, decided to become an artist.

Robert Jay Wolff left Paris and moved to Chicago with his first wife.

In 1933 and 1934 he won awards for his sculpture in juried shows at the Chicago Art Institute and had a one-man show of his sculpture. Then, once again embracing dramatic change, he turned his concentration to abstract expressionist painting in 1936.

The following year, he joined the American Abstract Artists. This artist-run group was formed in 1936 in New York City "to promote and foster understanding of abstract and non-objective art."[4] At the time the then-radical notions of abstract art were poorly received in establishment art circles.

Despite the criticism, the late thirties and forties were heady times for the American Abstract Artists, full of dreams and promise and daring and artistic camaraderie. Many of the artists had emigrated from the area of Eastern Europe that later became Hungary. Robert Jay Wolff made many life-long friendships from among this circle.

In 1937, a group of Chicago businessmen invited Walter Gropius (1883–1969), the German architect and founder of the Bauhaus, to set up a New Bauhaus school in their city. Gropius had already committed to Harvard and was living in Cambridge, so he recommended one of his colleagues from the Bauhaus, the Hungarian artist Laszlo Moholy-Nagy (1895–1946). Moholy-Nagy accepted the position and invited his friends György Kepes, whom he had known and worked with in Hungary and had shared a design studio with in London, and Robert Jay Wolff to join him. The Chicago experiment was short-lived but Nagy then opened his own school, the School of Design, in 1938. Robert Jay Wolff taught there. It was later reorganized as the Institute of Design and today is part of the Illinois Institute of Technology.[5]

The German Bauhaus school and movement was one of those rare convergences of highly talented people, as at Black Mountain and in Bloomsbury, where creativity sparked more intense creativity. Gropius's faculty members included Paul Klee, Josef and Annie Albers (who later founded Black Mountain College), Wassily Kandinsky, and students such as potters Franz and Marguerite Friedlaender-Wildenhain.

A core Bauhaus philosophy — form follows function — deeply influenced art and craft and architecture in Europe and the U.S. Though Robert Jay Wolff was never himself concerned with anything other than the fine arts, people whose work was steeped in the Bauhaus or who had worked in close proximity to it surrounded him. It is a philosophy that has influenced many American and European studio potters in greater or lesser degrees to this day.

The ceramics workshop at the Bauhaus lasted only five years and was physically separate from the rest of the school. There were tensions between Gropius, who wanted the workshop to focus on designing for industry, and his two ceramics teachers, Master Potter Max Krehan (1875–1925), who came from a long line of potters and taught everything from digging and preparing clay to throwing and firing, and Gerhard Marcks (1889–1921), who taught the history of ceramics and did not want the school to become a factory. Gropius himself designed a tea set, which is still in production, for the Rosenthal factory.

The Kepes, Breuer, and Chermayeff (Serge, 1900–1996) families all summered together in Wellfleet on Cape Cod. They entertained one another and there were great discussions about art and life and politics. The Wolffs could never afford to purchase a summer home like their friends, but they always managed to rent out their Connecticut house for a month or two, and borrow one of their friends' Wellfleet homes. By the time he was a teen, Wolff had a summer job on the Cape, playing drums at sock hops and yacht clubs.

The Chicago endeavor did not include ceramics, but underlying the many artistic experiments and undertakings of Robert Jay Wolff's friends was the stripping away of ornamentation and anything useless, which guided the Bauhaus movement.

Wolff remembers the artistic ferment that permeated the lives of his parents and their friends. "I was extremely lucky that I was born into this. There was all the drinking and smoking and it was pretty raucous: but I grew up around a batch of people who were completely driven to find something beautiful. They believed you had an obligation to follow your own potential, to follow your path to something true. Something new that was yours."

Robert Jay Wolff left Chicago to head the art department at Brooklyn College after the Second World War. He hired as his faculty Mark Rothko, Ad Reinhardt, Burgoyne Diller, Stanley Hayter and Carl Holty. While holding this post in Brooklyn, he attended a party in Connecticut and met Elizabeth Leighton, the Massachusetts woman who would become his third wife and Wolff's mother.

Elizabeth Leighton and her sister Constance (Connie) Leighton attended the private day school for girls that became Brimmer and May. Both sisters married men who were influenced by the Bauhaus movement and who became renowned architect-designers. Connie married Marcel Breuer. Their marriage endured and both Breuers were part of Wolff's childhood years. The Breuers had a home in Wellfleet and summered with the same circle of friends as his parents.

Elizabeth Leighton's first husband was Jorge Arango, the Chile-, Colombia-, and Harvard-educated Colombian architect. The couple lived in Colombia during World War II and had a son, Peter Arango (1946). After the war ended, they returned to the U.S. and divorced. Elizabeth then met Robert Jay Wolff, a dashing older man with a daughter from his first marriage, Wendy Wolff.

"She was adventurous," Wolff says of his mother, "interested in the arts, and everything around her. She was like a politician: anyone meeting her felt like they were the only person in the room. Her intellect was big."

As a young woman she had won a partial scholarship to go to Radcliffe but her family could not afford for her to go. She worked for Houghton Mifflin, the great Boston publisher during this exciting time, and had to write to her boss's friends in Latin. When Wolff was a "little kid, mother made pottery in the basement. She had a small electric kiln and took classes at Brookfield." But she devoted herself to his father's career. She saw her role as "taking care of the artist."

"There was a very vibrant community of thinkers in Litchfield County when I was growing up," Wolff says, "and for the first ten years of my life, I grew up with these people. I made a crossbow. Sandy [Calder] tried it and it broke. I was heartbroken. Sandy made me a new one.... At ten, I got interested in calligraphy and so Ad Reinhart helped me learn ... my father bought me German woodworking tools ... I was given the most incredible open road with two very informed adults making it as possible as could be."

Litchfield County, graced with the beautiful rugged highlands of the ancient Berkshires, nineteenth-century farmsteads and picturesque rivers, yet accessible to New York City, had become home to a circle of talented artists and writers who reveled in their creativity and each other. They socialized in each other's homes, threw huge parties, famously drank and smoked, and partied till dawn. It had become an informal artists' colony. To be a child in this community was to witness and also be influenced by it.

Peter Arango remembers the parties and says of his younger half-brother, Wolff, "As a little guy, much of his 'play' was imaginative and creative. He loved to make things from the start — banners, costumes, plaques, books. He loved tales of action and adventure, particularly those of knights and combat. He must have been about four or five when he made himself a set of banners and paraded through a gathering of grown-ups, all of whom were artists or writers — the Calders, Arthur Miller — making a sort of trumpeting sound. Louisa Calder, who was a professional grump most of the time, was enchanted and asked Guy if he was waging some kind of war. 'No,' he responded, 'I'm waging PEACE!'"

When Wolff was four, his parents realized that he "was walking into trees." His eyesight was poor and he suffered terrible headaches. He got his first pair of glasses but the headaches continued. He did not do well in school and stayed back twice in first grade. "My parents moved me around a lot," he says. He went to public school. He went to Rumsey Hall, the private school set on 147 bucolic acres along the Bantam River in Washington Depot. When he was in third grade, his mother desperately tried Calvert School homeschooling, a correspondence curriculum that arrived in the mail.

"Guy was a wunderkind from the start, as far as I recall," Arango says, "[But] he had terrible issues with his vision and was in and out of all sorts of diagnostic workups from the age of three or four. As a result, he was an active kid, a highly active kid, but not an athletic kid, until he took up skiing and bicycling, both of which he threw himself into with zeal . . . He was an avid (and skinny!) bike rider for years and actually invested in and rode a pennyfarthing monster bike; I was terrified he'd kill himself on it. He actually almost lost it all in a motorcycle accident in Wales — broken neck, terrifying, and part of his story as a musician [as he learned to play the banjo while recuperating]. Later on, although he remained an energetic skier, he became a fan of BMX bikes and built jumps near the pottery in Woodville."

When he was eight or nine, he visited Old Sturbridge Village, a living history museum known for its winding dirt roads, a wonderful collection of antique houses in various styles, a working farm, a bank, general store, sawmill, and gardens. Here, docents in period costumes replicate New England life from 1790–1840 by demonstrating early crafts and skills. Visitors can watch them dip candles, dye wool in iron vats, hammer hot iron into tools, and make barrels or tin lamps. Herbs hang to dry from the beams. Sheep and pigs and cows fill the barnyards and pastures.

"The buildings were inspiring because they were so beautiful. But something about the fact that people made what they used . . . that it was of the hand," affected Wolff deeply. "The last thing I saw was a man pouring hot pewter to make a spoon. When I came home I made moccasins. That was a moment for me, seeing that people could make their own things. Sandy [Calder] made me toys. But something about the fact that everybody could make their own spoon had an impact on me."

Back in public school in seventh and eighth grades in Washington, Connecticut, he had Ruth Pittman, at the time Ruth Prince, for an art teacher, "a spectacular finder of souls." He began to feel a bit more comfortable in school. Her daughter Susan had been Guy's best friend since he was in his elementary years. But his parents continued to be concerned about him and wanted to find a suitable place for his high school years.

In their circle, "everyone went to Putney," Putney School in Vermont. "It was the Andover Exeter of the art world." So his parents considered the prestigious and artsy private school for the next step in their son's education. Another possibility was Cambridge at Weston. Their friends Bill and Joan Talbot suggested High Mowing, in Wilton, New Hampshire, where a cousin taught. The Wolffs planned to visit all three schools.

"High Mowing was an architectural treasure of colonial and early republic architecture," Wolff says. It made him think of the houses at Sturbridge Village. The tables, the chairs, all the furniture was antique. There was a small room with Chinese wallpaper. Another had wide pine-board paneling with the original stenciling.

There's a vast hayfield that slopes down, away from the cluster of buildings that are the school, and if you stand at the edge of that hayfield, you can see out across the Souhegan Valley, to the rolling mountains that define the Monadnock region of southern New Hampshire. The school has placed a simple gazebo

The hilltop hayfield
that gave High Mowing
School its name.

nearby, with large-paned glass windows, for winter viewing. It is this field on top of a hill that gives the school its name.

Wolff knew immediately that this was the school he wanted to attend. He was drawn to the look and feel of it. It reminded him of Sturbridge. He and his parents had gone to see Cambridge in Weston but he knew he would not do well there. They did not bother to visit Putney.

Inspired by the writings of the Austrian philosopher Rudolph Steiner (1861–1925) and frustrated with the then-current state of education, Beaulah Hepburn Emmet (1890–1978), who taught art history and English at the Edgewood School in Greenwich, Connecticut, decided to set up a Waldorf secondary school on the grounds of her family's summer home and farm, High Mowing. Emmet's father was "a well-known New York banker, A. Barton Hepburn, who left a well-publicized estate of nearly $10 million when he died in 1922."[6] The family bought High Mowing in 1929. It consisted of the beautiful farmland acreage and a "long line of soft-grey, weathered buildings — built in 1763 and enlarged by David Cram in 1838."[7] The school opened its doors in 1942, during the war years when building a school was difficult because construction materials were allocated to the war effort. At the time, the New Hampshire authorities did not believe a woman could properly open a school and put many obstacles before Emmet, which, with determination, she overcame.

Steiner wrote and lectured about his ideas on many aspects of life, particularly his thoughts on farming, which coalesced into biodynamic agriculture; education, which grew into the Waldorf Schools in 1919; and living with disabilities, which became the Camphill movement; and included other ideas such as eurythmy, the art of expressive movement. He called the sum of his ideas Anthroposophy.

High Mowing, founded almost a quarter-century after Steiner started the movement, was the first Waldorf School in North America and remains the only one that is also a boarding school. "For the Waldorf student," the Association of Waldorf Schools of North America explains, "music, dance, and theater, writing, literature, legends and myths are not simply subjects to be read about, ingested and tested. They are experienced. Through these experiences, Waldorf students cultivate a lifelong love of learning as well as the intellectual, emotional, physical and spiritual capacities to be individuals certain of their paths and to be of service to the world."[8]

High Mowing interprets this mandate in their mission statement: "We aim to educate artistically through dynamic, transformative activity that resonates with the developmental stages of adolescence and the unique development of each individual. Inspired by love and respect for humanity and nature, our mission as a community is to recognize and nurture the highest potential in each young person, to foster the balanced unfolding of physical, social, moral, and intellectual capacities, and ultimately to awaken the will to make life choices with compassion and integrity."

It was not until he was a junior that Wolff realized High Mowing was a Waldorf School. "If you asked, they told you," he says. "But otherwise, they didn't talk about it." They embraced the precepts but wore the mantle lightly.

Wolff says that founder Mrs. Emmet liked his father but did not particularly like him. "I was too noisy," he says, "beating on my drums. I was boisterous." But Mrs. Emmet and the senior Wolff hit it off right away. And the senior Wolff very much hoped that High Mowing would help his son find his way.

"I knew I had to do well," Wolff says. "My parents were spending an amount of money that was not unnoticed. I had to succeed."

The ceramic studio is in the basement of the boys' dorm. The ceilings are low. The floors are cement. Along two outer walls, at shoulder height, there is a ledge for setting finished pots, a few geraniums, a stem or two of flowers, and behind the ledge, windows that let light stream in, making the space surprisingly bright. It's a well-thought-out studio, with lots of work tables, antique stoneware crocks for storage, both electric and kick wheels, an alcove that serves as the glaze room, an old farmhouse-style sink, a sturdy wedging table, and a few pieces of battered furniture. It is kept very clean.

Clay is reclaimed in large, shallow bowl-shaped plaster drying bats — there are no pug mills here. Students take their clay from these bats and wedge the clay into workability. It is a studio of simplicity.

When Wolff attended, the downdraft kiln, low-arched with four Venturi gas burners, built with two layers of firebrick and made pretty with an outer layer of common red brick, was at one end of the studio. This was convenient, of course, but some years after Wolff graduated, a horrified and perhaps overly skittish fire marshal discovered the not uncommon arrangement, a kiln in the basement, and ordered it removed — worrying about flames beneath the sleeping boys. It was torn down and rebuilt in a new and spacious wooden shed just a few steps from the studio. Here there are more worktables, stacks of kiln shelves, cones and other supplies. The shelves on the sides and back of the kiln are left in place from fire to fire. The front stack is rebuilt each time. Clay work at High Mowing, in Wolff's day and at present, is primarily stoneware fired to cone nine. Though

The stoneware kiln
at High Mowing School.

Wolff works primarily in earthenware in his own shop, he makes stoneware during his annual stay at High Mowing every February.

Mrs. Karl (Isobel) was Wolff's pottery teacher at High Mowing. She graduated with a BFA in ceramics from Alfred University in 1945 and came to High Mowing in 1946. A nonagenarian, she continues as the ceramics teacher as I write this. Deeply sympathetic to the Mingei philosophy (art of the people or folk craft movement founded by Soetsu Yanagi) and to the Waldorf principles of encouraging rather than lecturing, confident in her self-effacement, she requested not to be named in this book and refused to allow a camera near her. But she had a profound impact upon Wolff's life and chosen path, and no discussion of his ceramics is complete without Mrs. Karl. Indeed, she has nurtured a number of clay people.

"I lived in the pottery," Wolff says of his High Mowing years. "Because my eyes weren't so great I really took the tack that I would be working with my hands . . . when I was out in the world so I better learn how to do something.

The pottery was really the most interesting of the craft classes and I felt at first that I could learn about how to learn crafts by spending the most time I could, doing one. This kind of thinking was the gift that came from having the family I had and I know I was very lucky for it. I was hooked before I knew I was hooked. I had no less than two classes of pottery a day and often much more, plus time after school. I researched and immersed myself in what I considered was 'an apprenticeship.' I often say I spent four years, four hours a day making pottery at High Mowing. It sounds like a lot but it's pretty accurate; I was very in love."

Gordon Titcomb, the musician and children's book author, who has been friends with Wolff since childhood, and who also attended High Mowing, recalls, "He generally looked as if he'd spent the afternoon frolicking around in a mud-pit, which was, of course, exactly the case. His shoes, pants, and ever-present white tee shirt would bear the telltale signs of his long hours spent in Mrs. Karl's pottery studio . . . streaks and dustings of white and pink clay and glaze residue were always covering Mr. Wolff."

Mrs. Karl says of the innate talent she discovered in her young clay-obsessed pupil, "He was already a thrower before he touched clay."

"I loved High Mowing," Wolff says. "It was a beautiful environment."

"The great miracle for Guy . . . is that somehow Mom and Dad found High Mowing. Guy had been bullied and denigrated in schools — in part due to his vision issues and consequent learning issues . . . He is keenly intelligent and highly verbal, but schools had ganged up on him almost from the start," Arango says. It was "the one school in the world that operated in a way that Guy could enjoy. The Block system worked for him, and he met Mrs. Karl . . . High Mowing gave him great friendships, confidence in himself as a learner, new ways of expressing himself in music, and his craft. By the time he left High Mowing, he had become a wicked good drummer, a good potter."

Steve Fischer, another High Mowing student (now the Executive Director of the New England Booksellers Association) recalls Wolff as being a star, one of the most creative students in a school body that was largely creative. He was amazed that "there were kids my age who were really good at something and they were thinking that was how they were going to make a living. Before you could drive a car there was something you could do that was just you." Wolff was one of those kids. In fact, he was so good at pottery that Fischer assumed he had come to High Mowing already a proficient thrower.

When Wolff went home to Connecticut, he eagerly told his favorite teacher Ruth Prince (later Pittman) and his friend Susan Prince (Ruth's daughter) all about his new school. Taken with his enthusiasm and impressed with what the school had done for Wolff, Pittman decided to drive up to New Hampshire to see the school for herself. Wolff told Mrs. Emmet about his amazing art teacher from home, and his dad wrote Mrs. Emmet a letter about her. And coincidentally (or perhaps not), Pittman had already been introduced to the Waldorf principles

Thrown by Wolff, glazed and fired by Mrs. Karl, and decorated by her daughter Brigitta Karl. Cornish stone glaze, cobalt decoration.

by a professor and mentor at Southern Connecticut Teachers College (now Southern Connecticut State University). Mrs. Emmet offered her a job at High Mowing almost the moment she arrived, and so she and her two daughters moved to Wilton, New Hampshire the following autumn. Pittman joined the High Mowing faculty and taught art.

Mrs. Karl was influenced by the philosophy and teachings of Charles Fergus Binns (1857–1934), often called the Father of American Studio Ceramics, who as a founding director of the New York State School of Clay-Working and Ceramics in Alfred set the school on its course.[9] She was also influenced and inspired by two of her teachers at Alfred: Marion Fosdick, who taught pottery and sculpture, and Catherine Nelson, who taught painting.[10] And the British potter Bernard Leach had an impact on her. She brought these influences to her class and to Wolff, especially her interest in the work and thinking of Leach and his circle: Shoji Hamada, Soetsu Yanagi, and Michael Cardew.

Bernard Leach (1887–1979) published his seminal *A Potter's Book* in the U.K. in 1950, influencing generations of potters on both sides of the Atlantic. Leach discussed English slipware, stoneware, Japanese raku, and Oriental porcelain. His interest fused the English country traditions with the pottery being made in Japan and his admiration for Sung Dynasty ceramics of China. In his book, he gave instructions on everything from digging and processing one's own clay to making glazes and building kilns. He had strong opinions on what made a good pot. "In crafts," he wrote in Chapter One, "Towards A Standard," "the age-old traditions of hand work, which enabled humble English artisans to take their part in such truly human activities as the making of medieval tiles and pitchers and culminated in magnificent co-operations like Chartres Cathedral, have long since crumbled away. The small establishments of the Tofts and other slipware potters were succeeded by the factories of the Wedgwoods and the Spodes and in a short space of time, the standard of craftsmanship, which had been built up by the labour of centuries, the intimate feeling for material and form, and the common, homely, almost family workshop life had given way to specialization and the inevitable development of mass production."[11]

Leach made three tours of the U.S., lecturing and demonstrating; the first in 1952, the second and most famous in 1953 with Shoji Hamada and Soetsu Yanagi, which included two weeks at Black Mountain College and, later in the tour, a stint at the Archie Bray Center where Peter Voulkos kicked Hamada's wheel for him, and a third in 1961. In more than one instance, Leach let it be known that he did not think much of the pottery being made in the U.S. at the time, and blamed it on the fact that, in his mind, there was no tradition in this vast land. He seemed not to know about the rural potters in the southeastern states, multigenerational potters whose roots, as Wolff soon discovered, sprang directly from the same country pottery roots in the U.K. that inspired Leach, or the Native American pottery in the southwest.

The summer between his junior and senior year, Wolff followed fellow High Mowing School student and potter, his friend Sherry Erickson (now Travers) to Jugtown. Recollections vary on how the connection between High Mowing and Jugtown began. Erickson recalls that Mrs. Karl suggested she contact Jugtown. Mrs. Karl recalls that Erickson learned of the Jugtown apprenticeship and applied on her own. When the letter of acceptance arrived, she excitedly showed it to Mrs. Karl who saw that the director was Nancy Sweezy, her former neighbor and student (though Mrs. Karl demurs when called Nancy Sweezy's teacher, Sweezy claimed her as her first teacher).[12] Erickson, with Wolff close behind, was the first of a succession of High Mowing students to make the 950-mile trip to North Carolina to hone their skills at Jugtown.

Jugtown Pottery was a visionary project founded by Jacques (d. 1947) and Juliana Busbee (d. 1962) of Raleigh, North Carolina, during the first quarter of the twentieth century when traditional pottery, even in the rural South where it had lasted longer than elsewhere in the country, was in decline. Homemakers eschewed handmade crocks for modern glass canning jars and ready-preserved food in tin cans. Interest in seed pans, flowerpots, and other horticultural wares had dwindled. But when Juliana Busbee, wandering through the exhibits and booths of a country fair, saw an orange "dirt plate," an earthenware pie pan probably made by one of the early Owens family potters in North Carolina, she was deeply and emotionally affected by the honesty of the plate, its strength and simple beauty. She purchased it and brought it home to show her husband, who was also immediately smitten with the pie plate. Soon after, the two of them began to seek out and acquire more pieces. This was the first step in an important endeavor that did much to rescue, preserve, and promote the old ways of pottery making. Their work continues to influence potters today, and had a profound effect on Wolff.

What the Busbees discovered was a rich tradition of redware and stoneware pottery making, passed from generation to generation in the southeastern region of the U.S. Here, early settlers from Wales and England, with a rich pottery tradition behind them, found an abundance of plastic clays near the surface. They constructed groundhog kilns, great brick structures built into the earth like a woodchuck's burrow and fired with stacks of dry wood. They filled their kilns with the pots they had turned in the winter; jugs, churns, crocks, plates, washbasins, milk panchions, and quantities of horticultural wares.

Juliana opened a shop in Greenwich Village to sell the pots they purchased, while Jacques served as buyer, seeking out potters with wares to sell. Juliana was a brilliant marketer and the traditional jugs and jars and plates were a hit with residents of the artsy Village. But partially because the local potters did not quite trust the urban Jacques — might he really be a spy? — and partly because there were no longer many potters, it was difficult to obtain enough wares to meet demand. In 1917, the Busbees decided to start their own pottery in order to preserve the traditional ways and shapes before they were lost. They hired J. H. Owen (b. 1866) to throw, decorate, and fire pots which they sold in their Village Store Tea Room.

By 1921, the Busbees had opened Jugtown, named in the vernacular for all potteries that produced jugs for moonshiners. It was in a cluster of log buildings near the Owen Pottery in the picturesque Piedmont region of North Carolina. They hired Charles Teague (1901–1938) to throw for them. Two years later, Ben Owen (Benjamin Wade Owen, 1905–1983) joined them.

The Owen brothers, James J. Owen (1830–1905) and Joseph Owen (1823–1905), were probably the first members of this multigenerational family of potters to work in the Piedmont region, supplementing their farm incomes with pots they sold or traded to neighbors. "Families of artists are particularly exotic and appealing phenomena. The Owen/Owens family of Seagrove, North Carolina is such a family," wrote Charlotte Vestal Brown, who curated the 2009 show "175 Years of Pottery by the Owen/Owens" and is the director of the Gregg Museum of Art & Design at North Carolina State University in Raleigh. "Beginning with Joseph Owen (1823–1905) this extended family has crafted pottery for at least six generations."[13]

Juliana continued to run the retail shop in Greenwich Village until 1926, when the demand for folk pottery had become so robust that she was able to wholesale to other shops and no longer needed to operate one herself. She was now full-time at Jugtown, continuing to market, and doing some of the glazing and decorating. Jacques researched Asian pottery, and brought new shapes to Ben Owen.

Teague left to run his own workshop, but Ben Owen and the Busbees continued to work together in the cluster of log buildings. "For four decades this unusual collaboration between the Busbees and Ben Owen produced a folk pottery of great distinction. Describing a process as well as product, 'Jugtown philosophy' became widely known, establishing Ben Owen as a master potter and focusing attention on the area's potteries. Oriental shapes, produced with local materials and traditional turning and firing techniques, were assimilated into the local idiom and soon 'belonged' to Jugtown," Nancy Sweezy wrote in her first book, *Raised in Clay*.[14]

After the death of Jacques Busbee, Juliana Busbee and Ben Owen continued to work together until 1959 when Ben left to open his own shop, The Old Plank Road Pottery. A year later, John Maré purchased Jugtown and hired Vernon Owens (1944–) to "turn" (throw) the pots. Vernon learned to throw from his father M. L. Owens (1917–2003) and uncle Walter Owen. At Jugtown, he studied and imitated the robust pots that Ben Owen made, until he came to make traditional pots that were also his own.

"I just picked up old pieces and weighed 'em and guessed the clay weight, measured them and guessed about the shrinkage," he told Sweezy.[15] "I tried to make 'em exactly like the old pots, and that's where I went wrong. You just can't do that, it didn't come out right. It wasn't enough of me in the pots. 'Course I never had made that complicated a pottery either. People around here said the Jugtown pots, the shape, is so simple and all. They do look simple, but it's a whole different story when you go to make them. They are very complicated to make and make look right. You think it looks good, and a year later you see what is wrong with it . . .

"At first I just made the old Jugtown shapes. It never crossed my mind that we would make any other shapes. And what I had on my mind was whether the pot was too thick and what the color looked like. It wasn't until I took it over to run for myself in 1965 that I began to think, 'I'm making this pottery and I can't make it exactly like the old Jugtown. I need to make a good pot — similar — but let it be my pot.' I can't make somebody else's pot. Nobody did when they was making churns. Everybody had their own shape. That's why there's so many different ones around."

Vernon Owens worked for Maré and then, upon Maré's death, struggled to lease Jugtown from his estate. During 1968, the Cambridge potter Nancy Sweezy, former student of Mrs. Karl and later writer and folklorist, visited North Carolina with her mother, looking for locally made pottery for her Cambridge shop. She was dismayed at the condition of Jugtown and immediately decided to buy it. She managed to put together the funds to purchase the pottery for the nonprofit Country Roads.

In addition to being a potter, Sweezy was passionately interested in folk arts, and well connected. She had come to pottery during the fifties while living in Wilton Center, New Hampshire, near High Mowing School, with her three children and then-husband. While living in Wilton Center, she studied pottery with Mrs. Karl, her neighbor, at the Sharon Arts Center, at the time affiliated with the League of New Hampshire Craftsmen.

Vernon Owens stayed on at Jugtown after Nancy Sweezy arrived. During her tenure there, she developed glazes that were lead free and fired at higher temperatures than had been typical of the region. She also set up an apprenticeship program beginning in 1969, taking in more than 30 apprentices. She dramatically increased the visibility of North Carolina pottery and Seagrove bustled with potters from all over the U.S. and further who came to set up their own shops. Interestingly, the southeastern pottery traditions descended from the pottery traditions of England and Wales, and now, with the clustering of top potters in the area, modern English potters such as Mark Hewitt, whose father and grandfather were directors of Spode and who was himself born in the significant pottery town of Stoke-on-Trent, have relocated to Seagrove.

In 1983, Sweezy moved on to other interests and Vernon Owens bought Jugtown. But in the summer of 1969, when nineteen-year-old Wolff drove down to Jugtown in the red Volkswagen convertible his father bought him, she was the director. Sweezy and Vernon Owens were away at the Smithsonian the day he arrived but Vernon's father, Melvin (M. L.) Owens was around (M. L. is the one who added the S to Owen) and came over to see what new youngsters had arrived.

Wolff watched him make a candlestick. "It was architecturally impossible. He was taking clay and moving it in ways I had never thought as even a possibility . . . up, conical and tall. And then working from the outside, the second pull just on the exterior. By the end, it was lightweight, 6 pounds, 14 inches high. How is this possible? And on top of the stick, a bowl, above, compressed, a beautiful arch . . . one piece of clay . . . to a modern person would seem like magic. Completely impossible! It was hollow from bottom to top. Sort of like a trumpet and at the top, a delicate bowl, a place where a candle would happily stick into. That happened the first five minutes I was there.

"What I got right away was that that kind of pottery making was different from what the modern world was teaching; what the schools knew about, and that there was still a path that was kind of open." He sees watching M. L. Owens throwing the candlestick as one of the key moments in his growth as a potter. "From [my visit to] Sturbridge Village on I was really interested in why these early New England pots were so well made and had a vigor, had a life of their own. By my sophomore year I was collecting antique pots. When I went to Jugtown I saw why they were so good." He realized then that the quick, effortless throwing of a traditional potter gave life to the pots. Later, he researched the candlestick shape and discovered that it was a seventeenth-century Welsh form.

He stayed a month that first summer, gathered around a television with fellow Jugtowners to watch Neil Armstrong and Buzz Aldrin land on the moon, and then returned home and back to High Mowing. But Jugtown had connected with him, and he returned to visit, especially as other High Mowing students went down for apprenticeships. These included Tom Crimmens and Sharry Stevens-Grunden, who also spent time at Guy Wolff's workshop, Agnes Chabot Almquist, who returns to High Mowing every year to make pots for the May Day sale, and David Stumpfle, who set up his own pottery in Seagrove and attended High Mowing the same time as Erica Warnock, whom Wolff married in 1988, and Pam Owens.

Pam Owens, a student at High Mowing after Guy, and also deeply influenced in her clay life by Mrs. Karl, worked with Guy at his pottery for three weeks after finishing her studies at High Mowing and before going to Jugtown for an apprenticeship. On her mother's side, she is descended from the Hartford stoneware potter Daniel Goodale (c. 1840), the same Goodale whose work Wolff so admires. At Jugtown, she married Vernon Owens and continues to make traditional pottery there today.

Wolff runs a coggle just below the rim of a 24-pound full pot.

CHAPTER FOUR

Seeking the Old Masters

After Wolff graduated from High Mowing, he decided to go to Wales to seek out traditional potters. He wanted to immerse himself in their work, and to learn. Mrs. Karl, ever encouraging, wrote a charming handwritten letter of introduction punctuated with double and triple underlinings on High Mowing stationery that he was to carry with him, and present as needed.

JUNE 30, 1970

TO WHOM IT MAY CONCERN

Guy Wolff worked in a stoneware pottery here for four years. He started at the age of 16 — , an innocent, willing, cheerful and *hardworking* [underlined three times] beginner.

— I would not have accounted him exceptional at that time, except for his ability and willingness to work, with no expectation of reward.

Hard work, then, was the basis and very foundation of all his accomplishment. — But beyond this, Guy's vigorous and alive spirit, meeting with clay on the potter's wheel resulted in what we call, the natural, *Folk potter* [underlined twice]. *That he is*, from himself with no direction or earlier influence.

For a potter who reads this, I affirm that you have in Guy an unusually closely allied person with the materials with which you work, and that he has a unique value on this basis.

If he has occasion to use this letter as well, for other reasons, and as a general recommendation, I want to say that he is, beyond the ordinary, a *good*, and good-hearted person, one whom you can wholly *trust* [underlined twice], in the old, and former sense and meaning of that word.

MRS. ISOBEL KARL

As it turned out, he did not need the letter, but young and on his own, it was a comfort to have in his pocket just in case. He carried it with him, and keeps it still.

A friend of a family friend met a person who knew the proprietors of Haverfordwest Pottery in Pembrokeshire in the southwestern part of Wales, the Whalleys. This thrice-removed connection led to a job at the pottery. "Anything you do when you are twenty-one is important," Wolff says. "I was very fortunate that they took me. They were making contemporary pottery. The half badly thrown mugs were trimmed so the outside shape would match the interior. The bottom third had to be trimmed. I learned that I wanted to work differently. I learned what I wanted to do and what I didn't want to do." What he didn't want to do was trim pots. He wanted to throw pots. He wanted to start and finish their shape on the wheel.

His parents' friends, the Gabos, strongly urged him to go the Leach pottery while in England and Wales and offered an entrée. "Miriam Gabo and Naum

Gabo (1890–1977) — he was a sculptor, had moved to St. Ives … and they were there when Hamada came with Leach to set up their shop. So Miriam really knew them … So she said, 'When you go to Great Britain, you have to go to visit St. Ives and say hello to Janet for me.' I didn't go when I was working in Wales because the place had too much of an impact, it was too important to me and I was a little worried that I would get sucked up by the whole persona of the Leach thing, so I didn't go. I stayed in country potteries."

While he was working at Haverfordwest Pottery, his friend Sherry Erickson arrived from the U.S., also to make pots in Wales. The two young potters heard about the centuries-old pottery village of Ewenny and, intrigued that such a place existed, they decided to visit it.

Ewenny, near the sea in the south of Wales, has abundant good red clay, minerals including galena for glazes, and plentiful stone. Historic records indicate that potters were working in the area as early as 1427 and that, over the years, around fifteen potteries were in operation. The Ewenny Pottery was established by the Jenkins family in 1610 and has continued in the family for eight generations. Like the Owen/Owens family, the family potters sometimes established their own pot works, or worked for another local pottery such as Claypit Pottery. Ewenny Pottery was always owned by one of the Jenkins.

They produced lead-glazed domestic ware for everyday use in the kitchen and on the farm. They also took commissions for specialty items such as puzzle jugs. The Jenkins had a few kilns, one a now-famous 300-cubic-foot dome kiln, insulated and buttressed with stones. It was fired with coal and as it approached temperature, stoked with bundles of sticks. By 1958, the kiln had become too expensive to operate, and in the early 1980s it was dismantled and reconstructed at the St. Fagan Museum of the National Museum of Wales in Cardiff. Ewenny

From the collection of pots Wolff keeps for inspiration: grain jar, wood ash glaze on iron bearing clay, circa 1790–1820, 17 inches in height.

From Wolff's collection:
five-gallon stoneware crock,
circa 1860–1870, Albany slip
interior, cobalt decoration,
nice flat-ear handles, from J.
S. Taft & Company, Keene,
New Hampshire. Wolff
believes the potter had come
from Bennington but notes
the pot is "looser" than
Bennington pots.

From Wolff's collection:
stoneware jug by Daniel Goodale,
Jr., of Hartford, Connecticut.
Goodale, who potted during the
first quarter of the nineteenth
century, is one of Wolff's favorite
early American potters.

Pottery continues making traditionally shaped pots, with modern, glossy lead-free glazes.

After their visit to Ewenny, Erickson landed a job working for Eric Stockl who was renting space from Ewenny Pottery, in a building across the street. Stockl was an orphan, fifteen or so years older than Wolff, who had come to Wales after World War II. He was making traditional, Leach-inspired pots. Today he has a studio in West Yorkshire.

On December 5, 1970, Wolff hopped on his motorcycle to make the trip from his job at Haverfordwest Pottery to Ewenny Pottery to pick up Erickson. They were going to go to Cardiff to sell his bike. Wolff never made it. In a split-second life-threatening accident, his bike crashed and his neck was broken. Rushed to the nearest hospital, he was put in a body cast and told his recovery would take months. He would no longer be able to work at Haverfordwest Pottery. In hindsight, he believes this was fortuitous.

Eric Stockl, Erickson's employer, and his wife Meira, who at the time taught at Cardiff, offered to let Wolff stay with them and, as best he could in his condition, be a helper while he recuperated. He came as soon as he was out of the hospital and enjoyed the hospitality of the Stockls, playing games of chess and watching the first year of Monty Python. It was during this time that he learned to play the banjo, and, in his enthusiasm, bought banjos for his brother and for Sherry.

At Ewenny with the Stockls while recovering and doing odd jobs, he says, "I was very interested in what was going on at the Jenkins'. They were doing exactly what the Owens family was doing. They were making 45-second mugs. Mr. Jenkins made the foot with his fingernail!" Wolff was electrified. For the second time, he had an encounter with fast-throwing, multigenerational potters who made traditional ware in the old way. He wanted to do this too.

By March of 1971, he was recovered enough to go to Denmark to visit Abigail (Abby, 1952) Weisgard, his close friend from Roxbury, Connecticut. "We were

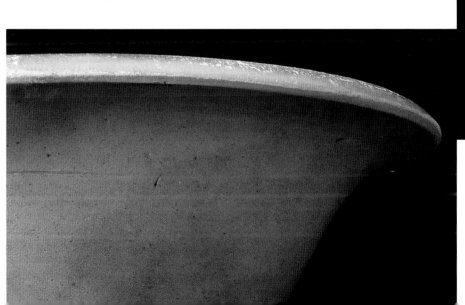

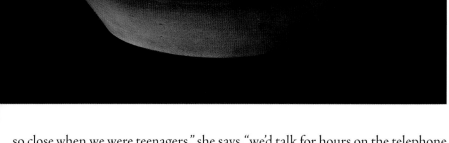

From Wolff's collection: joggleware Staffordshire cup, given to Wolff from a local collection. "Masterfully done," Wolff says.

From Wolff's collection: milk pan, interior glazed with Albany slip, from Troy, New York, circa 1820. This is Wolff's favorite bowl, especially the rim.

so close when we were teenagers," she says, "we'd talk for hours on the telephone about all sorts of things . . . he practically lived at our house . . . both my parents loved him like crazy."

Her parents, Leonard Weisgard and Phyllis Minot, left the U.S. in 1969 and moved to Denmark with their three children, Abby, Christina (Chrissy), and Ethan. Leonard Weisgard was a well-known children's book illustrator whose art graced more than two hundred stories. He won the Caldecott Award, collaborated with Margaret Wise Brown and numerous other top writers, and was the artist for many of the early Golden Books.

The family lived in a rented estate called Snoldelevgaard in the village of Snoldelev, thirty-five minutes outside Copenhagen. Denmark is famous, or infamous for its piggeries, and there was one next to the estate with "enormous" pigs.

"I remember Guy showing up on our doorstep wearing a gigantic white neck brace and my mother screaming!" Abby Weisgard says. The house was already filled with musicians. Guy stayed and ended up on the Danish television show *Mælk og Honning* (Milk and Honey) performing with Doctor Dopo Jam, a rock/jazz band. Wolff played conga drums like the "ones [he] played as a kid at the Calders' dance parties in Roxbury."

He returned home. He felt that it was time to start his own pottery and bring to the endeavor all that he had learned.

One might expect that if an abstract expressionist artist such as Robert Jay Wolff were going to produce a son who was a potter, it would be a potter such as Peter Voulkos rather than the potter son he got, steeped in tradition. Wolff disagrees. Instead, he sees similarities between his father and himself.

"My father was a classical thinker who was an abstract expressionist," he explains. "When I was first talking to the man who runs David Findlay, Jr. Gallery [the gallery representing Robert Jay Wolff], I said, 'I really think my father should be showing in London.' He thought I meant I would rather show [his works] in London than with him but what I meant was because of his classical methods, he would fit in — one of his paintings is at the Tate . . . What he did might seem contrived to a certain kind of Jackson Pollack thinker. My father wasn't wild. He was — well, that sentence of his, 'Tradition is not a form to be imitated but the discipline that gives integrity to the new' — a sentence like that really says it all, because an abstract person can find clarity and truth through understanding the materials . . . so it's all the same, that's really the truth. The route that one takes to get to something beautiful always has to come back to believing in the material and loving the material and hoping for the material the best it can be and my father was just as much of that thinking as me. Well, he gave it to me."

And what of the Bauhaus friends that surrounded his father? Did their philosophy have an impact on his father and hence himself? Bauhaus "is form follows function, but this is respecting the material, respecting the possibilities of the material. [My father] wasn't a wild guy. . . . His favorite artist was Claude Lorrain, who was a watercolorist of the seventeenth century. [He liked the] subtlety and the mastery that Claude Lorrain had in what he did. He loved Mark

LEFT
From Wolff's collection: slip-glazed, slip-trailed plate from Norwalk, Connecticut, circa 1820, 8.5-inch diameter. He believes it was probably made by Asa Hoyt or Absalom Day.

RIGHT
From Wolff's collection: redware pot, ovoid with wide mouth from Norwalk, Connecticut. Lead glazed with manganese splashes, circa 1820s, 10 inches.

Rothko's work, which again had wonderful subtext and quiet. He did not like Albers. With all the politest things to the Albers family I think of [his work] as being contrived intellectual exercises of color. My father worked in color . . . [he] was doing . . . landscapes without the landscape. He brought it down to just the essence of the colors. So there's *Slough Pond Nocturne* and *Slough Pond Dayturne* with big blocks of color . . . that were the elements of the colors of that place [Wellfleet]. So that's not haphazard.

"Voulkos is a very good person to bring up. I think it's great that there's been all of this sort of letting go and enjoying oneself. There's a big *but* going in here now. I remember a person coming in here [his workshop], who taught art in New York who said, 'I don't tell people what to do with the wheel, I just put them on and they do what they do.' To me that's like saying, 'I want you to write a poem. Figure out how to make letters.' If you don't give somebody some kind of framework to start from, how can they go anywhere? There has to be a framework that you are working from that you can let loose in. There's got to be something there." He shakes his head at the thought of no framework. "Boy, I've never been interested. It's just a waste of time. There's too much I want to know about the material. I want to be able to have a conversation with the material so I have to know something about it to be able to do that.

"Here's how extreme it is for me. If you go back to the southern English, what we call a pitcher and what they call a jug that has sort of a wet handle that . . . pops off the pot, that droops off the bottom . . . There's a certain kind of Cornish jug, a simple cream jug, and Devonshire-Dorset jug that has this handle that sits low and [these jugs] are *perfect* for the material. They came out of a world of earthenware pottery. This handle came from the nature of the earthenware clay. You can't get that languid handle from stoneware clay. Now the problem is around [the time of the] Leach family and a little bit later, people started doing that jug in stoneware and the whole reason for that jug is the way the clay *responds* in earthenware. So this is where I get in trouble, I say to people, 'That's a beautiful jug. I would like to see it in the material it was meant to be made in.' And most modern potters are going, 'What is he talking about?' So that's the thing, if you follow the material back to its essence, you then have to respect what it should be.

"So I saw a very nice David Leach pitcher from his family and I said, 'Oh this is beautiful, I wish it were in earthenware,' with all them being sort of shocked. 'Who is this guy who would say such things?'

"That's why I am so excited about Doug Fitch. Because he's of a place . . . he is really onto it. It's not for romantic reasons. It's for real practical reasons that you have to follow the material back and work from it . . . This is why I liked Hamada so much. He talked about a ton of different reasons: how do people find something that is of themselves and of a place and there are tons and tons of different ways people have to go about that. I think it isn't for any romantic reasons that he said 'of a place' but that you have to start from a grounded truthful environment for anything that you do . . .

"In Hamada's book he talks about going to meet that woman who had all those redware plates. That kind of stuff is really important." He is referring to Ethel Mairet (1872–1952), a weaver, and spinner, and supporter of crafts, and the dinner at her house that Hamada described in Leach's book, *Hamada Potter*. E. B. Fishley, who sold his pots at a nearby market, was a friend of Mairet's. Leach, Hamada, and Cardew visited her several times, and upon Hamada's departure for Japan, she gave him a wool suit that she had made from cloth she had woven. He wore it on his wedding day and many other occasions. Hamada describes the dinnerware: "When Leach and I visited Mrs. Mairet, the mother of English hand-weaving, in Ditchling, Sussex, she served us dinner using a complete set of slipware, which I have never forgotten. The dishes were products of Fishley, a potter who preserved the good traditions of England, the last one to do so. His slipware was often put on display in the market and sold there. The large and small pitchers, oval dishes, and green plates all went well with the large oak table. When you are invited to dinner by someone, you often notice, as a potter, that dishes of lower quality are used together with superior pieces. But Mrs. Mairet served food on the best dishes, a perfect score."[1]

Wolff turns back to his parents and their friends, "All these people were looking for truthful paths. That's a big gift to be given . . . I remember as a little boy, seeing Arthur Miller sort of devastated — well, you know you're at a party, somebody's drinking wine or something — the fact that he got attacked by McCarthy, that was like a wake for him. So you see somebody have that response and then they do a book about witches, you know. I mean there are serious things that happen in people's lives that are a first step. When I am talking to kids about art, I say everything starts with one motion and the real thing starts with a response to that motion. So something has to happen, it can be almost anything, and the response to that, and the architectural tension, happens from that, is the thing that makes for proportion and makes things exciting."

CHAPTER FIVE

Setting Up Shop

GUY WOLFF POTTERY

Back home in Connecticut, Wolff looked around for a place to set up shop. There was a barn on the other side of Route 202, opposite his parents' house in Woodville, that he remembered being vacant his whole life. A local summer camp owned it and agreed to rent it to him. He says there was a circular roller skating rink on his parent's property from the days of the Garland Estate, which had been there before the new road sliced through what became his family's backyard.

The story he tells is that "Miss Mary Pickford [1892–1979] rented the local guest house on the Garland Estate up the hill which had been a teahouse in the Victorian era. So she rented this teahouse and I guess Mr. Fairbanks came to visit. At that point it wasn't a marriage. It was sort of a love nest — her biographer stopped by and I asked her about the place in Woodville and her response was 'Shh.' . . . Miss Pickford . . . needed a barn to keep her donkey and her cart," while she lived in the guesthouse, so a barn was built for her, and that is the barn that became Wolff's shop. "Locally," he chuckles, "they always said it was built to keep Mary Pickford's ass."

It's a pretty barn, the wood of the vertical siding deep golden brown with age. There are two chambers on the first floor, and a loft that in later years he sometimes used as living quarters. The barn is built on a wooded hill that slopes down to the Shepaug River. It is close to the road, near a bend, and, in time, became a landmark.

Wolff believes that one's environment must be beautiful in order to do the best work. "Making your environment truthful," he says, "so the stuff that comes out of it is real . . . I have a sign up here [his current workshop] that says, 'No cell phones. No texting.' People come in and say, 'Oh do you have that up because you don't want people coming in and taking pictures and copying your ware?' No, the world is so bad at being present, yet if you don't leave some empty space for something to happen, or some silence, none of the magic will come out of the air. You have to leave space for the magic to happen. That's why Hamada had a beautiful Japanese house. It wasn't because he wanted a museum, it was the need to have really nice ground for the sparks to happen."

Wolff made the front of the barn his showroom, which he heated with a box stove, and the back his workshop. Aesthetically it was perfect, charming, but it was cold in the winter and hot in the summer. "If I dropped a piece of clay on the floor in the winter, it would be frozen within three minutes."

Wolff built his first kiln, a sprung arch kiln of soft insulating bricks, in the fall of 1971. He would, over the years, build five. Gerry Williams (b.1926) who the following year founded *Studio Potter*, the influential journal for working potters, came by several times on his way from New Hampshire, where he kept a studio, to the Brookfield Craft Center in Fairfield County, Connecticut. He would offer comments and advice on Wolff's kiln building.

His first firing was Thanksgiving weekend in 1971. If one uses the old terms, he says he would consider himself a journeyman at that time and that he was on a journey to learn more. Because the old-time potters were not allowed to use another source of power for their wheels until they had completed their seven and a half years as a journeyman, and he had not yet completed that time, he used a kick wheel when he started his shop. In his mind, he had not yet earned the right to use a powered wheel.

One of the first things he made and fired that year was a chess set for his uncle, Marcel Breuer. Breuer sent him a light-hearted thank-you note, written in bright red ink.

DEAR GUY,

As man to man, uncle to nephew, one citizen to another one, animal to animal: I thank you! I see the time rapidly approaching when the chess set will have an appraised value of $100,000.00, as an original oeuvre of that fellow, Guy Wolff — you know, whose statue is shit on by the Litchfield Commons sparrows — consequently a tax deduction of 50,000.00 plus, which only show how great you are! I was and am touched to the soft bottom of my rather rotten heart. I will nurse and keep that set — I will not sell it, even with a million dollar or ruble tax advantage! And I wish you frequent visit of your creative muse, on and on, blond, brunette or copperhead, skinny or mollett (better mollett, in the venerable tradition of our family!); also a happy new year and thereafter!

YOURS,

LAZKÓ

JAN. 2, 1971

In those days, he made pots and sold them so he could continue his quest to understand the old pots. When he had enough cash, he closed up shop and went off to visit traditional potteries in England and Wales. If he didn't sell enough pottery, he made music to pay the bills or for a time, did woodworking.

Gordon Titcomb describes the lively early years playing music in the shop, "He and I both got very seriously into Bluegrass and 'Old Timey' music at this same period in time. We'd frequently get together and share some newfound musical gem from a recording and then sit for hours and figure out how to play it. He and I, along with some other friends, made a couple of pilgrimages down to the great fiddlers' convention in Union Grove, North Carolina, during these years where we'd seek out the old, authentic banjo, fiddle, and mandolin players and glean as much as we could from them. The fact that both of us had

Northern accents as well as pretty long hair probably made it fairly obvious that we weren't exactly locals, but we'd generally manage to fit in enough to get into some jam sessions with a few of the old-timers and steal a lick or two.

"After we'd both graduated from HMS, we joined up again musically forming a band called Polecat with Guy on banjo & guitar, me on mandolin & guitar and our Litchfield county friends Mark White & Jim Stevens on guitar and bass respectively. Our myriad rehearsals would almost always be held at Guy's pottery barn in Woodville where we'd frequently entertain Guy's prospective customers with a song or two before Guy would put down his banjo and attend to the business of selling pottery. At that time, his pottery studio . . . the barn . . . had electricity, a wood stove for heat, and music 24/7.

Tamba stoneware
vase by Wolff, Barnard
washed with Seto,
14.5 inches tall.

"We continue to be great friends to this day and still occasionally get together at his new pottery and share a newfound musical treasure. Guy is a national treasure."

"I started off in Connecticut making interesting shapes that I thought were important and putting Albany slip on them. Then I started doing salt glazing. And I started doing a little slip trailing. I actually started doing white slip trailing on Albany clay first. Pure Albany slip and then Albany slip with little yellow decorations. And then from that to salt glaze and from salt glaze then to Cornish Stone, white with blue decorations on it. And combinations of those happened. And then I started doing what at High Mowing was called Seto. I was taking Albany slip and by half I was adding wood ashes. In the south they call it the Shanghai Glaze. We called it Seto because there was a Japanese version of that glaze. I don't know if it comes from Mrs. Karl being interested in Leach. I'm not quite sure where the whole thing about Seto came in. Our darker glazes we always called the Tamba glazes. The darker matt glazes. And the sort of sparkly, attacked by wood ash, iron-bearing clay glazes we called Seto. So you make combinations. With my glazes it's literally it's a cup of this thing and a cup of that. It's by volume whereas most people use a triple beam balance."

Wolff's work began to receive a bit of notice. Textile designer Eszter Haraszky chose his bowls, plates, jugs, and serving pieces for the illustrations in articles about her design work in *House Beautiful* and *Ladies Home Journal* in

1970. In 1946 she emigrated from Hungary where she had worked as a costume designer but turned to home design in the U.S.[1] She stayed for a time with Wolff's aunt and uncle, the Breuers, who introduced her to the young potter's domestic ware, which she thought went well with her weavings. In 1971 the *Waterbury Republican* published a photo of Wolff at his wheel and another of him playing his banjo. In 1975, Steven Reiner included Wolff in his piece "Here to Stay," published in the July issue of *Blair and Ketchum's Country Journal*. At last, in 1984 the *Hartford Courant* published a photo of Wolff drinking from a puzzle mug he'd made, and another of the mug itself. But in the nascent years of his pottery, his appearances in the media were modest.

In 1973, he went to the U.K. again. His then-girlfriend was very interested in English literature and wanted to make a pilgrimage to the literary sites. Happily, there were often potteries nearby. When she went to see the Brontes' house, he went to the Littlethorp Pottery, which began operations in 1831, making primarily tiles and bricks until the 1940s when they turned exclusively to traditional domestic and horticultural wares. When Wolff visited, the legendary thrower George Curtis was still running the pottery. He had begun as a bench boy in 1912, married the owner's daughter, and in 1939 inherited Littlethorp Pottery with her. He mostly made flowerpots. Philip Trevelyn did a documentary for the BBC in 1971 about George Curtis called *Big Ware*. He was widely considered the last of the big ware throwers. Note that there are several "last big ware potters" in England and Wales. In the film, he is shown making 60-pound flowerpots and ten three-inch flowerpots per minute. Two years after Wolff's visit, Roly Curtis, George's son, took over, but George continued to work in the pottery until he was 85.

Wolff traveled for the next few months, he and his girlfriend taking different routes, with her off to Scotland and he stopping to hear and play "homemade music." He had picked up an old John Gray banjo on Portobello Road, and began to wend his way toward Scotland, playing the banjo in pubs to pay for his traveling expenses. He stopped at the ancient market town of Penrith, in Cumbria.

At Penrith, he stepped off the train and "went into a pub and started playing music for people. On the wall there was a dart championship mug. It was an

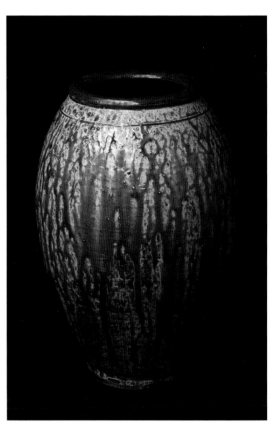

Wolff vase with Seto glaze, Albany slip rim.

Elizabethan slip-trailed posset [a pot for posset, a spiced drink made with milk that has been curdled with ale or wine]. On it was a recipe. It was an antique pot of the most beautiful type fired in an electric kiln. This was a pot that should have been in a museum but it was made by a modern person. I asked where they got it. And they said it was from one of the oldest potteries in the nation, down the way in Clifton Dykes called Wetheriggs, which means windy ridge.

"And so, the next day I walk out to this pottery. And I love this sort of thing . . . the potter is making mugs. It's early in the day. And I say to the guy 'that's a very interesting knuckling in.' And being an older term, I could see his antenna go up and he says how would you knuckle in and I said I come from the other side of the pond. He gave me 250 one-pound balls and put me on a wheel. I threw half by lunch. The potter asked me to stay. This was a guy 10 years older than me who bought the pottery. He had been at Findhorn and come south and met Harold Thornburn who ran Wetheriggs. They were a young couple, Joffy and Dorothy, taking on a traditional trade."

Wetheriggs was begun in 1860 after bricks and tiles were made on the site for the prior five years. It was near a railroad for transport and a river for steam power and boasted a good seam of clay. John Schofield (d. 1917) and Margaret Thornburn (d. 1937) had come to Wetheriggs from a potworks in Newcastle and the pottery remained in their family until 1973 when Jonathan (Joffy) Snell, the potter whom Guy encountered that first morning, came from Findhorn (the fledgling communal eco-village in the near-arctic north of Scotland), immersed himself in the craft, and later purchased the pottery.

Wetheriggs was known for its slip trailing. Harold Thornburn taught Snell and Snell taught Wolff to use a gravity slip trailer, made from a cow's horn with a bird's quill or an open clay vessel. "Gravity flow means you are not using a ball syringe, you are letting the clay pour out of a vessel and there's a quill coming out of the bottom, and they would let it pour. [Because], it's gravity flow [it is] coming out very fast . . . the way you would see somebody decorating with chocolate on a plate in modern times or coffee with cream decorations that people do. Very much the same kind of thing. So when I was at Wetheriggs I was doing that."

An unfired piece is covered with slip (liquid clay). Once covered with wet slip, the pot can be decorated with a few quick wipes of the fingers, or the slip trailer can be used to make cross hatches and vines and write names and dates. "Snell could make pieces like Thomas Toft," Wolff says. Toft was a seventeenth-century Staffordshire potter who slip-trailed unicorns, mermaids, pelicans, kings and queens, and his own name in intricate detail. Other Tofts, likely brothers and sons, also worked in the tradition. Little is known about Thomas Toft's life but the extant pieces attributed to him are of the highest standard and much admired. Snell's skill with gravity flow slip trailing informed Wolff's later work with jogglewares.

Wolff had a "wonderful" time at Wetheriggs and stayed about three months. While he was there, some people from Findhorn decided to stay overnight at Wetheriggs on their way down to London. They had with them a man named Paul, a new spiritual guide who had encountered the supernatural in the lush gardens of Findhorn, and whom they were eager to introduce in the city. It turned out to be Paul Hawken, whose company would years later purchase Wolff's flowerpots for the garden tool business Smith and Hawken, which Hawken co-founded in 1979. Hawken wrote about his Findhorn experience in *The Magic of Findhorn*, first published in 1975, and ignited interest in the movement in the U.S.

Wolff returned to his pottery in the Woodville section of Washington, Connecticut. "When I got back to the United States I did a lot of salt glaze work, and I would do blue decorations, and later on, because it looked a little too much like the old stuff, I started making a Cornish stone pot the way we had at High Mowing, so cone 10 with a feldspathic glaze that was very much like the Cantonese plates. The reason I did that was I was a little nervous that my pots were a little too close to the antique ones and the old ones were worth a lot of money. So around that period I started dating things and putting a little stamp that said Guy Wolff on it so people would know it was a modern pot. I found a few of my pieces in an antique store, which I found very disturbing. I started getting very careful about signing things.

"Just lately I've been talking to certain curatorial types on Facebook about really early joggled ware and that's so much fun. The big trick is you pour a layer of clay onto a flat surface and before that dries you slip trail on that. You couldn't do that with a ball syringe. It doesn't have the speed that you need that you get with the older method of gravity flow slip trailing. It's amazing what happens with these layers of the different slips that you wiggle around and you get these wonderful joggled surfaces.

"But to back up a little bit, when I first opened up my shop in America, the first thing I did was to put a slip glaze on everything. I did a cone 10 glaze with Albany slip and nothing else. I really wanted the shape of the pot to be the important thing. So it was rather ultra conservative to the extreme really, to just do one surface, either the pot was strong enough to hold itself up or it wasn't. I remember at one point Nancy Sweezy came up from Jugtown and she said, 'You have to get over this depression.' I just loved simple Albany slip, what an impact that made." Sweezy and Owen had stopped at Wolff's pottery on their way to Boston and spent the night in his father's studio.

Early saucered pot by Wolff, 4 pounds, 1993. This is the first type of flowerpot that he made.

"So after doing the Cornish Stone, then I started fooling around with low temperature. I didn't start doing earthenware right away but in 1976 I was going out with a young woman from Rockville Center, Long Island, and I went down to take her to her parents' house. And I kept seeing all these signs saying 'Garden Store' and I remember wondering, what are they doing in all these nurseries? And it just hit me that . . . if every potter in America started making flowerpots, they wouldn't be able to make enough to sell to Long Island alone. It's an immense market that all of us potters had missed seeing." He thought maybe it was the RISD or Alfred influence that had made everyone blind to the possibilities. And then he remembered that George Curtis of Littlethorpe Pottery had told him that if a Depression came again, "You can always sell eggs and flowerpots."

Back in Connecticut, "I said to Todd Piker, 'If we all started making these, we would not be able to keep up,' and he started making bowls for White Flower Farm, and a large part of his income came from it, large stoneware bowls . . . At Bennington in the 1850s they were making saucered flowerpots with a glaze on the inside. Sometimes just a little on the floor. In the early days they were salt glazed and because salt glaze doesn't let any water through they had to make an attached saucer with holes so the water could go out of this vessel. So I started making those first. And then I started working in earthenware and that's when I started doing the strawberry — there's a place in Georgia that makes strawberry pots — and I started making smaller strawberry pots just to get used to the material.

"So '74, '75, '76, '77 I was doing a lot of that and driving them down to Long Island. That would be my spring. So I made flowerpots in the spring and in August I would start making stoneware for my tourist summer sales and in the fall I would go back to England, not realizing that the biggest market was giftware for Christmas. But I slowly got into this thing that in January I would start making flowerpots for wholesale, and then in the spring I would make flowerpots for retail, and in the summer start preparing for Christmas really.

Except there's also a season for big flowerpots where people bring plants in, and they buy those in late August, September, and October. So the biggest market is making gifts for the leaf peepers, Columbus Day weekend, which for years was my biggest day of the year. It's now May Day but in the '70's it was Columbus Day weekend. Originally what I would do is work in the spring and in the summer, and in the fall I would go to England. I couldn't afford apprenticing . . . to go and stay with John Leach and work with him for a few years . . . I had a father who had a heart condition and they really needed me here and I had a shop going."

Throughout all these early years, at High Mowing, during his travels, wherever he went, Wolff looked at old pots: jars, crocks, panchions, platters, jugs, and, though he hadn't especially focused on them, flowerpots. All the traditional potters whose work he admired made horticultural ware in addition to domestic and agricultural ware. As we have seen, as other materials such as metal and then plastics replaced traditional earthen kitchenwares, the old-time potters turned more and more to supplying vessels for the horticultural market. Wolff had been looking at flowerpots for as long as he had been looking at early ceramics, though they had not been his major focus. Now he began to seek them out for study.

He continued to go back to High Mowing every year to work with Mrs. Karl for a week. He would throw pots for her to glaze and her daughter Brigitta to decorate, and Mrs. Karl would fire them and sell them in High Mowing's May Day Sale.

He also took in a few apprentices. One of those apprentices was Sharry Stevens (now Sharry Stevens-Grunden) who first encountered Wolff during one of his return trips to Mrs. Karl's class.

"Guy was a visiting alumni and teacher," she says. "He was using traditional English methods for making pottery, which means very quickly and surely, taking the pots right off the wheel. There wasn't any need for trimming the pots. I liked that a lot."

"I had one month with Guy after my junior year. The following fall I went to Jugtown for a bit. And then the following spring I went back to him and worked with him," she says, making strawberry pots. "I walked in while they were mixing a huge amount of clay and I got to help with that."

The clay was for Emmanule Rondinone, an Italian folk potter who had come to Bethlehem, Connecticut, to teach nuns in a convent to pot.

"So there's this one year when I couldn't go away, and guess what, there's this

Italian folk potter coming to the local convent," Wolff says. The convent was The Abbey Regina Laudis, in Bethlehem, Connecticut, which housed Benedictine women who were committed to manual labor, such as weaving, potting, and blacksmithing as well as agricultural work and scholarship. "There's a wonderful circle to all of this that's just so bizarre. At Alfred, when Mrs. Karl was there, one of the other people . . . was a guy named [Alexander] Giampietro. Giampietro also had worked at the Chicago Bauhaus where my father had been. He was a Washington, D.C. studio potter but he knew this Italian folk potter [he spent 1971–1972 in Italy on a Fulbright studying Italian folk pottery] and one of his daughters [Sister Perpetua Giampietro] was a nun at this convent.[2] So he brought this Italian folk potter over from the south of Italy, named Emmanule Rondinone. Now what's very interesting here, is his brother Vincenzo Rondinone had been brought over to Cornwall, Connecticut . . . back in the thirties and he had made estate flowerpots for all of the great houses around Millbrook and Litchfield County. So before the Second World War this Italian folk potter had moved to Connecticut and then later his brother came to this convent.

"By the time Emmanule came, Vincenzo was dead. It was just a coincidence . . . So what happened was a nun came to me and asked if I would prepare the clay for this Italian folk potter that was coming. I said, 'Oh yes please just as long as I can come and see it and learn from it.' So that was all fine. I made the clay. It's pretty intense, when you are not part of a community and it's a cloistered thing, it's problematic, and I am a person of the '60's, I had two apprentices working for me . . . Sharry Stevens-Grunden and Susan (Susie) Austin. Susie Austin ended going to Wisconsin and became one of the head throwers in Wisconsin Pottery. So here we are at this convent with this wonderful guy, who is the mayor of his town, who is probably four foot five or four foot eight, he's very short, and making a 32-pound lower section and a 25-pound upper section to make oil jars. Unbelievable! He was making three-foot jars. He himself was not five feet. The first thing he did was take a piece of clay and cut it in half and throw it together for wedging so there's this form of wedging. Everything that this man did was pre-Renaissance. He had a medieval pottery in a limestone cave in the south of Italy."

Rondinone threw a ball of clay into a wide ring, or short bottomless cylinder, and used that to affix a bat to the wheel head. He would remove the bat and pot, but leave the ring in place. Before putting the next bat down, he would level and smooth the ring. Other potters would smear clay on the wheel head with their fingers, or throw a flat plate to hold the bat. Rondinone's method was far more efficient. After that, whenever he uses a bat, which he avoids if he can, Wolff uses the method he learned from Rondinone that day.

Decades afterwards, speaking of the aging Italian potter's visit, Wolff still expresses wonder. "That's where I first saw [someone] making large low-temperature pots." It opened new possibilities for his own work.

"We were firing, throwing brush into this furnace that this man had made … To make a kiln, they made thousands of little bottles, so the firebricks are bottles, it's amazing, it's a whole other world. He had come and taught the nuns how to make these kiln liners, like bottles, and came back the next year to show them how to make them into a kiln. It was that kind of thing. So we were firing this kiln for the first time and there were all these flames and brush going in, and it was a different kind of brush than he was used to, he was used to olive wood … He should be a national treasure if he's not. It was problematic because those medieval guys really don't consider women important. He said about me that I was like a fish to water so he wanted to teach me so I could teach the nuns. I know what he was thinking: I was a lot further along so I should be able to teach them. He was probably 65 and I was 24 or 25 or 26, before Sharry went to Jugtown. It was a huge deal. There are moments in your life, it would be like someone who likes to play guitar having a few moments with Segovia. I got more information from him in the first two days that I met him than all the information I'd gotten in all the time up to that time, and that doesn't mean that I didn't learn a lot at Jugtown, it's just that it was so elemental. This thing of taking a large piece of clay and pushing down through it and wedging it, dancing on the clay to prepare it: all of those things. It was a huge deal to me. Seeing Vern Owens' father throw for the first time made me know that the reason for those pots still existed.

"After that I really was done with my trips. I needed to make money. By 1980 I'd gotten married. There were children and money to be made."

Grunden worked again at Wolff's pottery during the summer of 1975 and saved enough money to go back to the U.K. "I learned [from him] the western method of making pottery where you try to make the complete pot on the wheel rather than the generally speaking Eastern method where much of the pottery is trimmed, where you turn it over the day after or whenever it's ready. There is some great trimmed pottery out there but I really liked making the pot more complete on the wheel and cutting it off … [Wolff's] method of throwing, being that he can pick them up off the wheel, ensures that they are strongly made pots. I like his stuff a lot." Wolff gave her a map of places to visit and wrote a letter of introduction for her at Wetheriggs but she didn't need it. She was hired before the letter reached them and remained there for many years.

She too "learned a lot" from Snell at Wetheriggs. British law required that she had to return to the U.S. periodically. When she came back she would show Wolff what she had learned from Snell. When Snell came to the U.S., he too visited Wolff's pottery.

During his own travels, Wolff was seeking to understand how the great pots of the eighteenth and nineteenth centuries were made. If he could understand that, he could understand the New England crockery of his own area. He could understand the vitality of the pots. And it was that vitality that he wanted to achieve in his own work. "In the English pottery industry," he says, "apprentices were not paid until they could throw a half ton a day." That kind of throwing, he saw, was what gave their pots such energy.

Wolff had begun his professional career when the counterculture movement was near its height and protests against the Vietnam War had swelled to the majority opinion, with both dominating the evening news. *The Pentagon Papers* was published the year he opened shop and the war ended two years later. Wolff himself was exempted from the draft because of his poor eyesight.

Three Dog Night's "Joy to the World," Rod Stewart's "Maggie May," and Carole King's "It's Too Late" topped the music charts. *The Greening of America: How the Youth Rebellion Is Trying to Make America Livable* by Charles Reich hit the number one slot on the *New York Times* bestseller list in December of 1970 and remained number one for 20 weeks.[3] Also topping the *Times* bestseller lists for many weeks in 1971 when Wolff opened shop were *The Exorcist* by William Peter Blatty and *Bury My Heart at Wounded Knee* by Dee Brown. It was a time of self-reflection and rebellion and escape.

Richard Nixon was in the White House and, after years of the Vietnam War, inflation, taxes, and unemployment were at an all-time high. Nixon ordered a 90-day wage and price freeze, a move that was lauded by politicians on both sides of the aisle in hopes that it would help the challenging economy.[4]

The Back to the Land movement captured the imaginations of many young people and inspired them to eschew their parents' comfortable suburban lifestyles and buy or borrow plots in rural areas, where they worked at producing their own food. *The Mother Earth News,* begun in 1970, gave voice to the move toward self-sufficiency. The magazine instructed its readers on building their own shelters, growing and preserving their own food, utilizing alternative forms of energy, and a wide array of craft and country skills, including, on occasion, claywork.

Outdoor craft fairs appeared on town greens, in churchyards, public parks, parking lots, and fairgrounds around the country. The Handcraft Cooperative League of America and the American Handcraft Council joined forces to form The American Craft Council and held their first Craft Fair in 1966 in Vermont. The League, founded by Aileen Osborn Webb, had operated a New York City storefront, America House, since 1940. The Handcraft Council had begun publishing *Craft Horizons* in 1941.[5] In 1973, the American Craft Council moved the show to its legendary Rhinebeck location and held the first wholesale days in addition to retail days. Craftspeople, including potters, could now take enough orders from shops to keep them busy for a year, and earn a modest living from their work. Later, the ACC started the first indoor winter show in Baltimore, again with wholesale days.

Wolff did the first Litchfield Craft show "for fun" and then no shows until the big garden shows in the late nineties. Going his own way, he did not participate in the proliferating craft fairs and never participated in Rhinebeck. He concentrated on selling from his own shop, but like much of his generation, he was inventing his own way of life.

"Today, when Guy is a celebrated potter and the notion of enduring tradition has gained some traction," his brother Peter Arango says, "it is hard to remember how original his vision was in a time of relentlessly 'revolutionary/ radical' creativity. His aesthetic was with him from the start, and he is actually much more like Calder as an artist — a playful mind in a malleable art — than like Dad, who had a very serious notion of the 'rules' of art."

Philosophically, the American crafts movement descended more from the British Arts and Crafts Movement than from the Bauhaus, yet it was potters from the Bauhaus Movement, many of them expatriates fleeing the rise of Nazism in Europe, whose work influenced mid-century ceramics in the U.S. They were the teachers. Pottery moved into the academy.

The Arts and Crafts Movement, founded by William Morris, was a reaction against the impersonality of the burgeoning Industrial Age and the cold precision of factory-made goods. Morris extolled the superiority of good design, simplicity, and excellent craftsmanship. The Bauhaus, also honoring simplicity and good design, embraced modernity and the factory-made, and sought to form a partnership between artists and industry.

After World War II, many returning veterans seeking to take advantage of the GI Bill, which paid for college tuition, turned to crafts rather than engineering or the liberal arts. With their new degrees, they were able to obtain teaching jobs as more universities offered courses in ceramics.

In 1953 *Ceramics Monthly* began publication. The early editions were focused on how-to articles, profiles of potters and of studios, history, and readers' suggestions. In 1971 when Wolff opened his pottery, there were stories on whether lead glaze is safe, raku, how to make a slipcast ocarina, how to make a slip cup, throwing covered pots, a profile of Herbert Sanders and more. *Ceramics Monthly* continues today as the most important ceramics publication internationally, though there are other fine magazines.

When Wolff opened his shop doors, *A Potter's Book* by Bernard Leach was in its twelfth U.S. printing. *Pioneer Pottery* by Michael Cardew was published in the U.K. in 1969 and the U.S. in 1970. "I loved the pictures in Cardew's book," he says. "I really liked Cardew."

Michael Cardew, Leach's most famous student and later colleague, was particularly taken with the English slipware tradition and sought out the old country potters in the West Country. He admired the jugs, washbasins, mixing bowls, and other domestic wares they threw at great speed and in vast quantities in their shops. He sought to emulate the energy of their pots in his own. He learned to throw from William Fishley Holland of the legendary Fishley family of potters, and persuaded Elijah Comfort to come out of retirement and work with him. In time, he was able to throw lively pots himself, including big ware. "The paradox of spontaneity is that it very often springs forth most readily from an arduous discipline," Cardew told the critic Garth Clark.[6]

Mrs. Karl had introduced Wolff to Leach's ideas when he was at High Mowing. "Mrs. Karl . . . was of the Binns tradition . . . They all [at Alfred] understood the impact of how important Leach's book was and his direction. He was pretty much on a pedestal when I was a kid in school." She also introduced him to the work and ideas of Shoji Hamada and Soetsu Yanagi and the concept of Mingei.

"I am very, very grateful to Bernard Leach for showing us all Japanese pottery. And I was really happy and thankful to Michael Cardew. The thing about Leach is that he sort of translated and talked about these wonderful handmade goods and his book is a huge deal, very, very helpful to us all. He's kind of a person who drew and then made some pots . . . I think he would be one of the first persons to say he wasn't a very good potter."

Some years later, Wolff got to meet Cardew when Cardew came to visit Todd Piker at his pottery in Cornwall Bridge. After graduating from high school with a passion for pottery, Piker had gone to England to apprentice with Michael Cardew at his Wenford Bridge Pottery. He set up Cornwall Bridge Pottery with his friend and fellow Cardew apprentice Svend Bayer about fifteen miles northwest of Wolff's pottery in 1974, just a few years after Wolff opened his shop. "We did a very, very thorough search around the country for clays that we thought would be appropriate. We chose New England because this is where the wood was. I do wood firing. But that meant that finding clay was going to be a challenge. The advice was to go where the clay was. The reality being what it was, and the property being up here, plus there was a lot of wood for firing. So I had clay shipped to me from all over the country. We wanted to do stoneware. But we didn't have a kiln to fire the tests in. And I met Guy and he was really generous with his eagerness to share ideas and be a part of what we were doing. He really was excited about this large wood kiln that we were building. He was very interested in wood firing at the time. It didn't end up being what he did. I think he did a little bit of wood firing. He stayed with the earthenware and fired it electrically but we continued to fire with wood in a very large production pottery, which is very much in keeping with Guy's idea of the way in which folk pottery is done. That's what is significant — he was so accessible and so willing to be helpful . . . over the years he and I have had multiple experiences. How fortunate it was to have met him when I did."

Wolff talking to Michael Cardew at Todd Piker's Cornwall Bridge Pottery, outside, near Piker's kiln. Courtesy Guy Wolff; photographer unknown

Piker and Bayer built an enormous, multichambered wood-fired kiln in 1974 based on kilns Bayer had seen in Asia. Cornwall Bridge continues to produce a wide range of beautiful domestic ware.

That night, while standing outside near Piker's kiln close to where Cardew was also standing, Wolff tells us, "I was saying I would rather have the European way of one decision instead of seven decisions," meaning he'd rather fire a one-chamber kiln than one with many chambers, "and because of that we started to talk about Winchcombe which is where he was making redware. Ray Finch was there. I said as only a twenty-something-year-old would, 'I wish I was there when you were at Winchcombe.' His response just made me respect him twenty times more than I had before I met him: he said, 'Yea, I never threw a good pot after Winchcombe.' And with many apologies I agree with him. And this isn't about heritage or this or that. Because with redware, in Great Britain . . . because of the material, there were certain shapes that happened. So there's a

The dome kiln that Wolff built at his Woodville studio with bricks recycled from a New York bomb factory.

whole group of people in England making certain shapes that should be made in redware in stoneware. They don't have the same meaning as the original piece because they are shapes that are contrived into a shape that happened naturally with the red clay. So Cardew's early redware pieces are really really exciting. He could have been the great potter of Great Britain, so because of that I am slightly saddened but I also really respect him for what he did. I respect both of them for what they did."

Piker says, "Cardew always said he stopped making earthenware because it was much more difficult. People think earthenware is easier because the temperature is low, but in fact getting glazes to melt, the range of maturing of an earthenware clay is so narrow that if you don't get it just right, there's bloating."

In the summer of 1980, Wolff built a dome kiln for his salt-glazed pots. "I was doing salt glaze and I was working from Bernard Leach's book," Wolff said explaining his decision to build a dome kiln. He realized that "bottle kilns that went up, the updraft ones . . . used a lot of fuel," so "not having a lot of money" he decided to build a downdraft "because it cost less money to run. So I built a salt kiln with a six-foot dome. There was a factory over on Route 22 in New York State that had made the bombs that hit Dresden . . . they used magnesium,

I think . . . and there were these high, high temperature bricks, there must have been three football field lengths of 8 or 10 foot tall circles of hard bricks. So I bought a nice new Chevy pickup truck that year and I spent three months bringing 2,000 bricks back from that site. The guy would let me in. Todd Piker got bricks there. Other potters went there. I can't tell you how many kilns must have been made of bricks from that site."

He built the interior of the kiln entirely of the bricks he had collected and recycled from the bomb factory. He then covered the kiln with a blanket of insulating ceramic fiber, a product that was originally invented for the space program but had recently come on the market for potters. He ordered a truckload of used red bricks for a third, outer layer, much as the kiln at High Mowing had an outer layer of common red bricks.

Wolff fired his dome kiln to cone 10 (2340°F) with propane. "Some nights it took 600 gallons to reach temperature." Hard bricks are extremely dense. They heat up slowly and hold heat for a long time. They are very durable and can withstand even the rigors of a salt fire. Salt glazing can deteriorate soft, insulating bricks but kilns built of them fire more quickly than a kiln built of hard brick. The dome kiln, though beautiful to look at, and capable of producing wonderful pots, turned out to be very expensive to fire.

Over the years, he built four sprung arch kilns of soft brick, the last one a cross draft. "I call it my fast fire kiln," he says. "The flame hops across and then is pulled up the chimney. It is run on a positive atmosphere . . . the burners have blowers and a short stack. The big kiln is a negative atmosphere kiln." Today, he hopes to take both the dome kiln and the sprung arch down and rebuild them at his current studio but the task would take precious time away from his pot making.

Thus his early professional years he spent working in his own way, making salt glaze and Albany-slip-glazed stoneware, large jars and vases, and earthenware strawberry pots and saucered flowerpots, producing large amounts of pottery in his picturesque but cold-in-the-winter, hot-in-the-summer barn. He continued his quest to understand the vigorously thrown old pots. It was difficult but he was doing what he wanted to do. He was making the most honest pots he could. He was moving the material. He did not, however, enter juried shows. He did not make sculpture or political pots. He made no appearances in the ceramic press.

CHAPTER SIX

A Passion for Horticultural Wares

One day, in the first of a confluence of serendipitous events, a woman stopped at his shop. "She said, 'I worked with all these old antique pots at Kew and I miss them. Could you make some?' And I was very flippant with her the way one without a lot of money can be when people come to you with great ideas [for things they want you to do], and I said jovially, 'Get me an order for $3,000, and I will research it and teach myself how to do it.' And I thought she would go away."

The woman was Tina Dodge, from the Tiffany family, married to Michael Dodge, who worked at nearby White Flower Farm for 26 years. She too was associated with the prestigious nursery and had studied and worked at Kew Gardens. Wolff was about to be thrust into the world of very serious gardeners who had a great, unmet need for beautiful, well-made pots.

"So the next day she came back with an order. One thousand of it from Tim Mawson, and another thousand from Joe Eck and Wayne Winterrowd who were doing Tasha Tudor's garden. So I didn't wait for three. Two was good. And I said, 'Great, I'll start.' So I started working on them . . . She loved English gardening . . . She was really a fine, traditional gardener, and was now doing gardens for the distinguished garden historian Timothy Mawson."

Mawson, who was British, opened Timothy Mawson Books and Prints in an old cider mill in nearby New Preston, Connecticut, in 1984. He specialized in rare and antiquarian books on English gardening and was widely respected as an expert. The *New York Times* called the bookstore "influential."[1] He wrote *The Garden Room*, published in 1995, the year of his death from AIDS at the age of 54. When he was working with Smith and Hawken, Wolff did a commemorative pot celebrating Mawson that benefited AIDS research.

Joe Eck and Wayne Winterrowd created their oft-visited gardens, North Hill, in Vermont and together and individually wrote books and articles. Eck continues today. Tasha Tudor, the award-winning children's author and illustrator, was also known for the romantically old-fashioned way she lived in a reproduction Cape house built by her son in Vermont. She was also a serious gardener.

"We asked him to do a firing of pots from drawings by Tasha Tudor and they were a complete failure. They systematically destructed. Every pot cracked. And we obviously were not happy and he was not happy and he said, 'May I try again?' and we said, 'Sure, Guy,' and then he produced a magnificent set of pots. Largely on English models, long toms and things like that and we have been buying pots from Guy ever since."[2] Looking back and reflecting on this early experience in their 2009 book, *Our Life In Gardens*, Eck and Winterrowd wrote, "about fifteen years ago we met Guy Wolff, and our whole pot habit altered. For he was willing to make hand-thrown clay pots to antique designs, and that is what we wanted. It must be said that the first experiments were not a success, but quickly Guy came to understand this medium, new to him, and the pots grew finer and finer. Now, working from historic fragments, his pots are without compare, and our collection is enriched year by year.

"Among the many models he makes, our favorite perhaps is taken from the portrait of the myopic young Rubens Peale, painted by his brother Rembrandt, in which Rubens lovingly holds an old clay pot with one of the first pelargoniums grown in America. It is a scrawny thing, and Rubens, though charming, is not precisely a handsome man. But the pot is beautiful, and its reincarnations under Guy's hands line our greenhouse benches and when empty are displayed on shelves in our potting shed. We will never have enough of them."[3]

English full pot, the shape we often think of when we think of flowerpots; 12 pounds, 2012. Here Wolff has coggled his name under the rim.

With "creative activity, things happen out of themselves," Wolff says, speaking of this move to serious flowerpot making. "I was interested in old stoneware and earthenware pieces made in the eighteenth and nineteenth centuries," asking, "Why are they so good? What makes them so wonderful? While I am looking at old pots . . . going to the Connecticut Historical Society, or looking through Sturbridge Village's collection, or . . . private collections, besides a nice jug, people have a flowerpot or two. So it isn't that I went looking for [flowerpots] as a thing, but it happened organically that I got a background in, oh this was happening at Bennington in this period and in Hartford they were making this sort of crock, and oh look this is the same thing as a flowerpot because it's going outwards, same handle and it must be made by the Goodwins because it looks like a Goodwin handle. So none of the facts that I have in my head are at all academically obtained."

Instead he learned by looking closely at the pots, becoming familiar with each potter's style, inhabiting the potter's hands across the centuries. Pots, handles, rims, the line from the foot to the rim differ, sometimes ever so slightly, from locale to locale, from workshop to workshop, from potter to potter. He was looking closely at these differences. Seeing a pot, he looked for its similarities to others. "It is from the joy of the throwing and the respect of the beautiful pieces . . . that I say, 'Oh I think this is a Hartford.'" Wolff sought out and looked at paintings and etchings with pots in them, at old pots themselves, and at shards. Friends and even people he didn't know began to look for old examples. There were no books on the history of the flowerpot. The literature was scant. He was relying on primary sources.

"When Tina Dodge came, I did that first full pot." This is the classic flowerpot shape, with a simple slightly thickened rim, wider at the top than at the

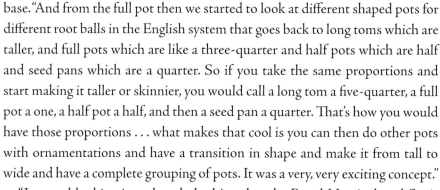

Long tom—for plants
with long taproots and
for topiaries—in white
clay with mineral-
highlighted beading and
crown, 4 pounds, 2012.

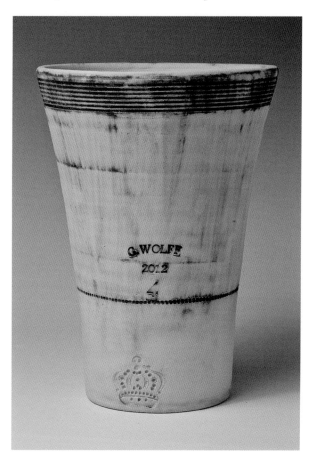

base. "And from the full pot then we started to look at different shaped pots for different root balls in the English system that goes back to long toms which are taller, and full pots which are like a three-quarter and half pots which are half and seed pans which are a quarter. So if you take the same proportions and start making it taller or skinnier, you would call a long tom a five-quarter, a full pot a one, a half pot a half, and then a seed pan a quarter. That's how you would have those proportions . . . what makes that cool is you can then do other pots with ornamentations and have a transition in shape and make it from tall to wide and have a complete grouping of pots. It was a very, very exciting concept."

"I started looking into the whole thing that the Royal Horticultural Society was coming up with: different shaped pots for different root balls in the greenhouse. Around 1805 they came up with this idea that you would make very wide pots to very tall pots for different kinds of root balls. So the system goes," he reiterates, "the tallest pot, which is very long, is called a long tom for a tap root, and then there's one that's slightly taller than it's wide that's called

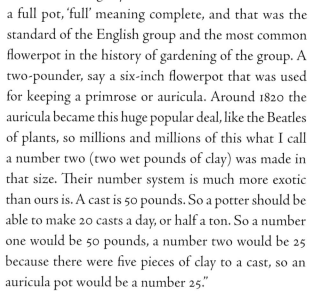

a full pot, 'full' meaning complete, and that was the standard of the English group and the most common flowerpot in the history of gardening of the group. A two-pounder, say a six-inch flowerpot that was used for keeping a primrose or auricula. Around 1820 the auricula became this huge popular deal, like the Beatles of plants, so millions and millions of this what I call a number two (two wet pounds of clay) was made in that size. Their number system is much more exotic than ours is. A cast is 50 pounds. So a potter should be able to make 20 casts a day, or half a ton. So a number one would be 50 pounds, a number two would be 25 because there were five pieces of clay to a cast, so an auricula pot would be a number 25."

"So long tom to full pot. Half the proportion of the full pot would be called a half pot. So, long tom, full pot, half pot. Half of a half pot is this wide pan, what we would consider a flat today, and that was called a seed pan. A seed pan without holes was then a bulb pan. Then with seed pans, they had starting pots. There was a thimble, which was about the length of a thimble that goes on your finger, thumbs that were the length of

Peale full and half pots, white clay, 2 pounds, 2012.

a thumb, and rose pots that were about four inches. Starting pots, which were thimbles, thumbs, and rose pots. That whole group I called the English work pot collection. I don't have a connection to the Royal Horticultural Society. I would love to be able to say this is the RHS system but that would take a licensing that I don't have the money to do. Of late I've started putting a crown on the pots of English origin. I went to the mall with my daughter. She found a key chain with this little crown, so I have been stamping the side of the pots with a crown for all the pots that come from this English system. It's to celebrate that they're from England. It might be a little pompous but it's fun.

"So after finding the English pots, I started looking at this whole ornamental thing and then I found the *Rubens Peale with a Geranium*. After the Rubens Peale, there's this grouping of Georgian pots, we have *Rubens Peale with a Geranium* 1801, we have Monticello, the one with the dots, and then we have one from Mt. Vernon, which has fine dents and then serpentine reeding around the side. We have John Bartram, which is very simple, that has fine dents in the lower rim, just has an understated serration going around."

He and his friend the garden writer, historian, and authority on houseplants, Tovah Martin, discussed flowerpots and their shapes and looked at and for pots together. She told him that "plants didn't come inside until 1833 — well, I don't know the exact date, but the date that's important is when America invented rolled glass, because rolled glass meant that windows could get bigger and cheaper." Tovah Martin told Wolff that "gardening came inside with that. I remember going to the Massachusetts Historical Society and seeing *Rubens Peale with a Geranium* — the important thing about all this is, we started looking at ornamental flowerpots in American gardening and I saw that picture and I said that's 1801, and I thought, oh, I can show Tovah that she's completely wrong. I went back to her and I said, 'Look, here's a man with a plant inside in 1801, and she said, 'Guy, I wasn't talking about the American elite who have been planting inside since the 1700s.' The popularity of bringing things in didn't happen till later."

Wolff threw the pots for Mawson's order and carried the wareboards outside to the open air so the pots would dry more quickly than if he kept them in the shop. The boards, with the freshly thrown flowerpots, were visible from the road. A "fellow drove past in a truck and skidded to a stop. His name was Ken Selody and he was a young topiary man from New Jersey who was getting things from White Flower Farm to take up to a very famous gardener named Allen C. Haskell of New Bedford, Massachusetts. So there was this . . . week and a half period where I went from not making flowerpots to having this nice man who [is working with] Mrs. Mellon [who is flying] in to get his topiaries," and with Allen C. Haskell, stop and fall in love with the newly made flowerpots.

The nice young topiary man, Ken Selody, owns the seven-acre Atlock Farm in Somerset, New Jersey, specializing in showy container plants, coleus, and most of all topiary. His work regularly appears in gardening magazines.

Allen C. Haskell was widely respected in the horticultural world. Accomplished gardeners from Europe and around the U.S. made pilgrimages to his eight-acre New England garden planted with rare, unusual, and often ancient specimens. The Queen of the Netherlands imported hundreds of topiaries from him. Jackie Kennedy asked him to help with her daughter Caroline's wedding.[4]

Mrs. Mellon, who had ordered the topiaries from Selody, was Rachel "Bunny" Mellon (b. 1911), the garden designer who redid the White House Rose Garden for her friend Jackie Kennedy and who reputedly owned more than 10,000 botany books.

All that Wolff knew of his new customers was that they were serious about their gardens and garden design, and they liked his pots. "It was just the luck of the draw that I got picked up by the who's-who of the garden world, first, before anything else. I didn't know that at the time. I just knew people were coming to get flowerpots." Selody still sells Wolff's hand-thrown pots at his nursery. He and Haskell each developed relationships with Martha Stewart, appearing on her show, and Selody became a contributing editor for her magazine.

Then Kathryn Meehan, a garden historian, the owner of Terra Cottage Garden Living and at the time assistant chief of horticulture at the Smithsonian, sent him some pictures of flowerpots she had collected. "She had a great collection of old pots. She really kicked the door open for me." By now Wolff was putting photos he took or that others sent him into albums. Her photos were an extraordinary addition to the personal reference collection he was building. "That's when I learned about Solomon Bell and Samuel Bell . . . Solomon and Sam Bell are really important to me. And this really great potter who was also a sculptor, German, who lived in Maryland and Virginia, Anthony Baecher . . . These were sort of ornamental pots and they were exciting and I started, you know, working from them . . . country potteries started making ornamental flowerpots . . . between 1850 and 1870 . . . still being handmade . . . but they are sort of innocently making them more ornamental so the nice housewife who is getting one will think it's pretty indoors instead of just an outdoor pot."

Wolff was producing a rich variety of comely flowerpots himself, inspired by these artifacts and images that he discovered or that were shared with him. His Maryland Rim, which he also calls his Baecher flowerpot, is inspired by the work of Anthony Baecher, who worked in Maryland and in the Shenandoah

Valley of Virginia in the last quarter of the nineteenth century. Baecher produced "many richly glazed flowerpots, vases, and wall flower holders as well as large urns for yard display."[5] He was primarily a sculptor and made figures that are highly collectible today but he also made great quantities of earthenware pots, particularly flowerpots. Wolff especially liked a flowerpot Baecher made while in Maryland "in the 1870s that had a particular split rim that is joined together. It's just a wonderful pot." Wolff's Maryland Rim pot is enhanced with the same ornate rim. Often, the sole decoration on these old pots and on Wolff's is in the rim.

Wolff's Jefferson Pot has a Georgian double rim, impressed with what he calls "dots," which are small roundish indentations in each rim. It was inspired by shards found in the kitchen garden at Monticello.

The Mount Vernon flowerpot, also Georgian, has a double dent on the rim and serpentine lines that sweep across the body, and reeding along the base. Wolff explains that when there is one line, it is a line, two is a bead, and three or more is reeding.

Wolff's Hartford Pot is inspired by a mid-nineteenth century pot that Elizabeth Fox, curator of the Connecticut Historical Society, showed him. The CHS has a wonderful collection of early redware and stoneware, including almost a dozen earthenware flowerpots. Wolff found inspiration in all of them. One of

the flowerpots has two upside down U-shaped handles, flat against the wall of the pot like those put on crocks, making it comfortable to lift and carry.

Joe Eck gave Wolff a similar flowerpot from the (Moses B.) Paige Pottery in Peabody, Massachusetts. Peabody, Massachusetts, and nearby Danvers, boasted 75 potteries at the start of the Revolutionary War. The Paige Pottery operated from 1876 until 1950, when it burned.[6] As with the pot at the Connecticut Historical Society, the Paige pot has flattened handles and a thickened rim. Wolff does not believe that early English and English-descent potters folded their rims over, but rather threw the pots to be thicker at the top.

"Years and years of looking at collections and old pieces and along the way you come upon things," he says referring to the pot he saw at the Connecticut Historical Society, "that had a rounder rim so that's probably 1850 by the way the rim looks and the heft of the handle . . . And then you see the same kind of pot [from another shop] and they were making exactly the same pot, but transformed . . . by what else is going on in that shop and the clay at the time. So by 1870 the rim is a little straighter, the handles are a little bit flatter, maybe they just cut a piece of clay and rubbed it in."

The Peabody, then, has the same proportions as the Hartford, but is modeled after "a pot that was found in a Salem, Massachusetts, garden," which he believes was made by the shop in Peabody, "because there's a picture of a pile of those pots [there], made somewhere between 1888 and 1890 and 1920 . . . And it's obvious that that pot was made for a very long time in that area because there are a lot of them. You can find them in antique stores."

The Ackerman Pot, coggled, with an attached saucer, was inspired by an illustration in *Ackermann's Repository of Arts, Literature, Fashions, Manufacturers &c*, published monthly from 1809 to 1829 by Rudolph Ackermann (1764–1834) in London. Wolff saw an Ackermann illustration in a small New York hotel and was intrigued, as it was from the same time period and style as Jane Austen. He began to look for more Ackermann illustrations, and thinks that Susan Tamulevich found the magazine with the illustration of flowerpots. "There's a woman leaning against a table and on the table are three flowerpots that are all rather inspired by what one would call Greek things, the whole romance around Greek design. And there are decorations on [the pots] that I put on my pots, that may just be shadowing on the woodcut. I don't know if it's a decoration or shadowing."

The Brandywine Pot, in white clay, was inspired by Henry DuPont's collection. It has a Chinese bowl shape, flared, with a Tuscan rim and regency decoration. It sits on three feet, which he makes separately. "I was combining things I like," he says.

The Enid A. Haupt Conservatory, at the New York Botanical Garden, was the inspiration for the Conservatory Pot. "I wanted to celebrate the structured lightness of glass," Wolff says. The pot has vertical flutes that he makes with his fingers while the pot is still wet on the wheel.

Pots made at the Jennings & Wagdin Pottery around 1874 in Galena, Illinois, the lead-mining town that Ulysses S. Grant called home at the time, are the inspiration for Wolff's Galena Rim flowerpot. Wolff's pot has a complex, ruffled, triple split rim. The July 2013 issue of Better Homes and Gardens' *Country Gardens* features Wolff's president's pots, including the Galena for President Grant.

Triple ruffled Galena
rim pot, redware,
inspired by pots found
in the lead-mining town
of Galena, Illinois; 4
pounds, 2011.

Phil Eichler of the Urban Gardener in Chicago began looking around for old pots for Wolff, and sent him photos. Another pot inspired by ware from the region is one he calls a Truro, based on his hunch that the form was brought over from Wales or England. He makes it in white, rubbed with minerals, red, glazed and splashed with oxides similar to two flowerpots found at chs, but the original was in gray clay. His has a crown ruffle rim. "There is one from Devon or Dorset or Cornwall, my own guess is that it's Lake's Pottery in Truro in Cornwall. This is where I start going, 'Well, I am not sure I am correct.' There are styles and the way it's thrown. One of the strongest reasons I think it's from Truro is it's the same shape pot being made in Galena, and Galena was peopled by people from Cornwall and Wales. And both Truro and Galena are lead mining villages. So the fact that there's a lead mine village in Illinois peopled by people from Cornwall, and it has that rim and then there's that rim from the Cornwall/Devon/Dorset area. I would love to get on a plane and go look for that pot and find one that says Lake's Pottery on it. It's just a guess that's in my head. So now that pot is called a Truro for me. That's in my head. It may not be true." Lake's Pottery, founded by W. H. Lake & Son in 1872 in Truro, closed in 1980 after suffering a fire several years before. Bernard Leach admired this shop and sent students to visit.

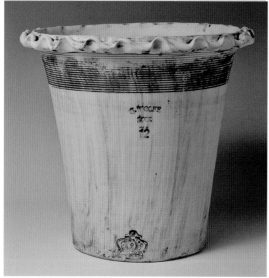

Asked what his favorite flowerpots to make are, Wolff answers, "Because I am a New Englander, I really like to make a Hartford or a Peabody with the handles. Because I am a crocker, I make crocks with little ear handles. There's a certain group of New England flowerpots that just have those handles. I really like the Rubens Peale Geranium flowerpot, that Georgian pot with a rope. I have always loved that pot.

"So there are all these different shapes that kind of show themselves all over America. The thing that's kind of fun about them is they are all rather innocent. And North Carolina has a different way of doing a little bit of fluting on the top rim, that's slightly different again. Here in Hartford again in the late 1700s, early 1800s, there's a really bent-over flute that's pretty and on the bead below or the rim below the top rim has what's called in the industry 'fine dent.' There's heavy dent and fine dent. Those are done with a wheel that imprints with little up-and-down lines all the way around. You see that on the handmade plates from the eighteenth century [Connecticut redware plates are famous for it] and you see it on the edges of flowerpots and you see it on mugs, about half-way up they would do a fine dent. It's a typical late eighteenth century, early nineteenth century decoration."

Wolff continues with his inspiration list, speaking the names fondly as if recalling old friends. He loves these pots and has a deep intimacy with the way the potters moved the clay. "Daniel Goodale of Hartford, probably something like 1813 up into the 1830s, Frederick Carpenter from the same period in Boston is a huge deal for me, I really like Peter Cross who was a Dutch potter in Hartford. He was making stoneware. Remember we weren't allowed to make stoneware before the Revolution, so there was this huge push for people doing salt glaze right after the Revolution." Connecticut was not blessed with stoneware clay. Only earthenware can be found in the state. But there were rich stoneware beds in Long Island and New York, as well as the most famous in South Amboy, New Jersey. Once the embargo was lifted, it was not too difficult to ship quantities, usually via boats on the Thames and Connecticut Rivers, to Connecticut potteries.

"Of course I love the Crolius family of New York. And being from Connecticut — this part of Connecticut — Litchfield County is right on the edge of the German Dutch potters on the other side of the Hudson, and then the English potters being in Hartford, Litchfield, Goshen, Lyme — people down in Norwalk. There was another Dutch potter in Greenwich, Adam States, and his potting descendants in Stonington and Norwich. There were redware potters in the eastern part of Connecticut very early on, 1690s, 1700. I have a pot upstairs that's from that group that's incredibly beautiful . . .

"So the thing that's so exciting about a flowerpot is that the transition in the line of it has all that exciting stuff of — [as] with all good pots — a beginning, a middle, and an end . . . The line of the old English flowerpot — that they made millions of — has a slight arch and then there's this doming thing that goes up towards the top, and right near the top, it bows out a little bit. So, if you were to look at it very offhandedly, you would see a straight line, but there's this subtext of a very powerful architecture for frugal reasons: the pots can be stacked in the furnace because the architecture makes them strong enough to take the foot of the next one inside and the foot of the next one inside and the foot of the next one inside [this would enable more pots to be stacked in the kiln, and save fuel]. So being that I was that interested in the architecture of pots, I realized that there was a reason for this pot to have this slightly simple addition to this line — but what it also does is breathe all this life into the thing."

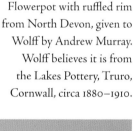

Flowerpot with ruffled rim from North Devon, given to Wolff by Andrew Murray. Wolff believes it is from the Lakes Pottery, Truro, Cornwall, circa 1880–1910.

Yet, he believes the pot should take backstage to the plants. "The pot has to disappear. The pot is the secondary actor. The plants coming out are the ones coming out and doing this soliloquy." He points out that the pots change once they have been filled with soil and planted. They acquire patina, maybe moss. Though they are beautiful the moment they come out of the kiln, age makes them even more beautiful. Like gardens, flowerpots are a four-dimensional art form, changing over time.

Wolff continued to work quietly at his workshop, throwing 24,000 pots a year and becoming more and more of an expert on the history and aesthetic of the flowerpot form. Increasing numbers of gardeners made their way to his door. The *Cincinnati Enquirer* did a piece on him and, though it was a one-city paper more than seven hundred miles away, it broadened his audience. In November 1991, Frances Chamberlain wrote a profile in the Sunday *New York Times*. Wolff told Chamberlain, "I don't copy old pots but have spent 25 years finding the architectural reason why they're made."[7] He is shown, his trademark bandana tied around his head, standing in front of his pottery; in his shop flipping a flowerpot over to dry; and holding a large jar. There is a close-up of his hands as he spreads a large piece of centered clay on the wheel.

Two years later, in July of 1993, *Victoria* magazine published Tovah Martin's piece, "Potter Guy Wolff's Quest to Master The Dance of the Hands." It was a two-page spread with eight color photos of Wolff's flowerpots and antique flowerpots. "Although Woodville, Connecticut is not on many maps, savvy gardeners brave country back roads in search of Guy Wolff's pottery. There, in a humble studio, Guy turns out terra-cotta so similar to old English flowerpots that antiques dealers sometimes confuse his handiworks with century-old earthenware. Each G. Wolff pot, custom crafted to nurture roots, is the result of years of apprenticeship."[8] She goes on to give an account of his life, managing to include, in the colorful prose she is known for, his childhood, his trips to country potteries in Wales, and his philosophy of making pots. "Able to discern an antique flowerpot's pedigree the moment he touches it, Guy runs his deft fingers over the clay's contours inside and out, he taps the walls to hear the ring they make, and he lays the earthenware against his cheek to sample its texture. The clay divulges not only when and where it was thrown, but also the tempo of the potter's wheel that gave it form and the type of plant it was crafted to cradle. For a moment, clay and craftsman commune."[9]

Toshi Otsuki shot the photos for the *Victoria* piece at designer Bunny William's trendy New York City shop, Treillage. Williams, who spent 22 years at the decorating firm of Parish-Hadley Associates, had gone out on her own in 1988. She co-owns Treillage, "a garden furniture and ornament shop," with antiques dealer John Roselli. When the *Victoria* piece was published, Wolff's flowerpots were available at Treillage, at A. C. Haskell's and at other well-known gardening meccas, as well as at his own pottery.

Suzanne Portero, a buyer for Smith and Hawken, the popular mail-order catalog and growing chain of retail shops that catered to gardeners who demanded high quality and good design in their tools, outdoor furnishings, and horticultural apparel, read Tovah Martin's piece while flipping through *Victoria* magazine in her dentist's office. "She called up and said we'd really like to work with you. Being that I'm a small little shop I said, 'Do you know what you are saying here, you have this huge company, I'm one guy, I will give you my life, I will make flowerpots for Smith and Hawken forever, but there's only so much that comes out of this shop.' She said. 'It's worth it, we'll do it.'" Paul Hawken, who had founded the business with Dave Smith, had stepped down and then sold Smith and Hawken. Though their paths had crossed during Hawken's Findhorn years, Wolff's and Hawken's paths did not cross now. Wolff, with years of practice throwing quickly and repetitively, a spiritual descendent of the old-time tonnage throwers, began making as many flowerpots as he could for Smith and Hawken.

The spring 1994 Smith and Hawken catalog, with its romantically sepia-toned cover, offered a Long Tom at eight inches, a Half Pot at six inches, a Pinch Pot at five inches, and an urn at eight and a half inches. The copy reads, "More than pleasing to the eye, the contours of a Guy Wolff pot encourage plants to grow by providing room for their particular root shapes. Tall and narrow, the Long Tom offers ballast for lilies and other plants with deep taproots. Species that produce a root ball, such as pelargonium, are comfortably settled within the traditional nineteenth-century English Half Pot. The Pinch Pot (its rim shaped by thumb and forefinger like the crust of a pie) shows off herbs, pansies, and our Midsummer Madness collection. Modeled after an eighteenth-century Tuscan design, the rope-bottom urn is well suited for campanula, lobelia, and other flowers that will spill over the sides."

The pots are pictured clustered together on a gravel walk, some nested, some on their sides, two planted. In a sidebar, the catalog effuses, "His pots do not sit silently but beckon to be filled . . . Gardeners take to the heft and roughened texture of his pots, which settle into the garden more readily than their mass-produced distant cousins."

Wolff had been throwing flowerpots for Smith and Hawken for about six months when an executive from Smith and Hawken visited his shop on her way to the New York Gift Show. "The CEO was then a woman who had gone to Wesleyan, on the rowing team, and she pulled the door handle off! And she said, 'This is more important than just the pots. People have to see where they are being made, because you know it's a pretty little barn.' I'd been there for a few decades at that point, and the whole story they found interesting. Smith and Hawken decided that they wanted a really good photographer to come and take pictures so they hired Richard Brown who is the big deal for garden photography on the east coast. When *Horticulture Magazine* heard that Richard Brown was coming to my shop they called him up and said, 'May we do an article on him at the same time and pay for half your day?' So it meant neither Smith and Hawken nor *Horticulture* had to pay for the whole thing. I changed my shirt in the middle of the shoot. We did some for Smith and Hawken and we did some for *Horticulture*."

And then, on a December afternoon in 1994, Martha Stewart gave Oprah Winfrey a special Christmas gift while appearing on the *Oprah Winfrey Show*. It was an amaryllis planted in a pot she had purchased at Wolff's shop. He does not remember Stewart coming into his shop; because he did not watch much on television except movies based on Jane Austen novels, he would not have known who she was. But the next morning, his phone began to ring nonstop. Viewers called him from all over the country. They wanted his flowerpots.

Reminiscing in her blog in 2009, Stewart wrote, "I first encountered Guy when I was traversing Litchfield County in Connecticut in search of antiques, plants, and ideas for the magazine. Ensconced in a small wooden building, Guy was busy making flowerpots for gardeners like me. He explained that inspiration came from history, paintings, and his own artistic imagination. I was quite taken by his pots and became a 'regular' customer."[10]

The following summer, someone from Stewart's show "called and said we want to do this show on your flowerpots . . . I was divorced from my first wife, but she had left me one of Martha Stewart's cookbooks, you know with the Laura Ashley dresses, and I actually said," he shakes his head in disbelief, "to one of the production people, she should not wear one of those Laura Ashley dresses, she will get dirty in here, and they said, oh no, that was years ago."

The show, a "field trip," was taped at Wolff's studio and called "How to Make a Terracotta Pot." Martha chatted with Wolff about his flowerpots and he explained to her the English system of specific pot-shapes for various types of root balls. He demonstrated throwing for her, and though this was his first experience working in front of a television camera, he was so comfortable sitting at his wheel with his hands in clay, so much himself, that he appears completely relaxed. He then took her outside and showed her his kiln. It had cooled down enough to unstack. Martha was astonished that he had to unbrick the door each time, something most potters must do. "You mean you have to unbuild yourself?" she exclaims. Wolff is standing inside the kiln. She asks for one of the pots, and taking it in her hand, admires it, taps it to hear it ring and then asks how one would go about ordering his pots.

The show and *Horticulture Magazine* appeared within a week of each other. One of Brown's photos of Wolff's flowerpots, lavishly planted, was the January 1996 cover of *Horticulture.* Inside, in his four-page essay, "Feat of Clay: Potter Guy Wolff puts a new spin on an old art," Oliver E. Allen describes Wolff's studio as a "somewhat ramshackle structure next to a busy road," but he is enchanted with the simple beauty of Wolff's pots and imagines them gracing gardens everywhere if only people can find them. Watching Wolff throw, he is mesmerized. "Now, swiftly, with one hand on the inside and the other outside, he lifts the low wall of clay up, up and out, guiding it and shaping it unerringly until suddenly, the pot is very close to its final configuration. This critical phase is called 'springing the form' and is the essence of the art: while bringing the clay up has given it the same thickness throughout . . . no mean feat."

Having his flowerpots featured on the cover of *Horticulture* was a lightning bolt in Wolff's potting life. "The day that *Horticulture* came out I got a call from the nice lady, Peggy Cornett, Curator of Plants, that gardens at Monticello. And then this wonderful woman who inspired and has helped the Philadelphia flower show happen named Diana Strawbridge Wister called. Diana ordered a batch of pots. The guys at Monticello said, 'Let's work together.' And then Steve Jobs

FROM LEFT TO RIGHT Regency decorated hothouse pot, 2 pounds; English half pot with cross-hatching, 6 pounds; and Baecher rimmed half pot, 2 pounds.

called. That was a day! The whole thing just broke into another world. It was about a fifteen-minute period, to talk to the most prestigious garden museum in the world, the nice lady with 2,000 acres to fill with flowerpots in Philadelphia and, you know, one of the great men of the century was pretty amazing."

Jobs' first words when Wolff answered the phone were, "Where's the nearest airport?" He said that he wanted to fly his gardener out. Wolff had no idea whom he was talking to or if it was a joke. Jobs had not introduced himself. But indeed he did send his gardener to Connecticut. The gardener brought photos of Jobs' home so that Wolff could design the pots to go with it. He placed a large order.

"A lot of that job I failed because we had a lot of humidity that year. Me learning to make bigger pots in such a humid year was just a disaster." Wolff has now devised a special way to fast-dry big pots by flipping them over onto plastic and setting them under a ceiling fan, but then, he was working in the traditional way of leaving them on ware boards. Jobs could not understand why it was taking Wolff so long. He did not understand or want to understand that pots need to dry and big pots take a long time to dry, especially during a muggy summer. He wanted the pots ready for a party he and his wife Laurene Powell were planning.

"But what was interesting about that making," Wolff says, "in Palo Alto they had this wonderful Arts and Crafts house. The house is exactly what we would all want . . . handmade. It had an arched ceiling, a handmade slate roof, with a transitional curve to it. The gardener came with a ton of pictures, so I designed a pot that had the transition of that roof, and finished off with the dome. So the pots that I made for that house, I used the look of the property. The architecture of the property was the inspiration for the pots that went onto that land."

Despite the delays, Jobs liked the pots he received and placed them in the garden. In August of 1997, the photographer Diana Walker, who was the White House photographer for *Time Magazine* for twenty years and who became friends with Jobs during a shoot in the early eighties, took a photo of Jobs and Powell sitting on a bench in Jobs' garden, surrounded by Wolff's pots, planted with hydrangeas. The photo was featured in *People Magazine* after Job's death in October of 2011.[11]

Then, on March 19, 1995, the *New York Times Magazine* ran a photo of Wolff's pots on the cover. Wolff was a solitary potter working in a rented donkey barn where he had worked since 1971, a man fascinated with and knowledgeable about eighteenth and nineteenth century pottery, a potter throwing enormous amounts of clay, making humble flowerpots. And then, unexpectedly, and quite

suddenly, gardeners all over this country and beyond wanted to put his flowerpots in their gardens and on their patios and in their homes. "It was a decade
and a half or two decades of preparation, and then it became a roller coaster,
very, very quickly," Wolff says.

"Being that I grew up with people that had so much celebrity that nobody
ever met them," he says, explaining what helped him with his encounters with
famous people like Martha Stewart, "I understand how untouched by human
beings people that are really famous are. Arthur Miller was a very lonely guy
because nobody ever wanted to meet *him*, they wanted to meet the guy who
wrote *Death of a Salesman* . . . in 1956 someone wants to talk to who you were
in 1940. It gets pretty boring pretty fast . . . I had sort of a slight odd skill about
not taking the celebrity at face value. It's not important. You still have to meet
the person to find out who they are. It's nice what you do but who are you? And
that's [worked] well. You just get a more fulfilling interaction with interesting
people if you do that."

But his own "overnight" celebrity was more challenging. He could throw
quickly and with assurance. He had the energy to work long hours. But he could
not make pots for all the people who wanted them. The demand was more than
he, no matter how prodigiously talented, could handle alone.

CHAPTER SEVEN

The Guy Wolff Guilds

After the life-changing results of that year, Guy Wolff recalled, "With Martha and with Horticulture, that's when the relationship with Peter Jackson had to happen. Wholesale-wise I could probably make $125,000 worth [of pottery] a year. So with a company like Smith and Hawken, that's times three. So when they started ordering about a million dollars worth of stuff, that's impossible."

Historically, potters have not always worked in solitude. A solitary potter who performs all tasks, throwing, decorating, firing, selling, packing and shipping, is a construct of the studio potter movement. Early American potters often worked in small groups, two or three brothers, or a father and son, or sadly, in the South, a slave owner might have slaves such as Dave the Potter throw pots for them. Sometimes whole families worked in the pottery. In the heyday of the era in which the English flowerpots Wolff loves were being made, there were workshops and guilds staffed by numerous potters: apprentices and journeymen. Both Leach and Cardew produced production ware with apprentices and skilled potters. There is a deep historic precedent for potters working in groups. Those traditional potters who had worked alone in their later years, such as Button, were forced to by circumstances.

Regency decorated pot,
white clay, 4 pounds, 2012.

Wolff felt very strongly that though there was more demand than he could meet, he did not want to enter into a relationship with a factory where pots were never touched by a human's hand. He wanted his pots to be individually handmade to the designs that he had researched and developed. He had to find a way to get help making his hand-thrown flowerpots.

" I could try to start a shop in Connecticut," he says, but he knew he did not have the personality to be a boss. "I can't. I can't," he says. "I am not a good taskmaster. I am not a good babysitter. You know people have messy lives and when you take on people they are getting married; they are getting divorced; they are getting sick — you know all the things that happen in life. I am not a good Boy Scout leader. I'm too emotionally involved in everything I do. I can't be neutral about stuff."

"Guy and I met about '86 or '87," Peter Wakefield Jackson says. "We had a mutual friend at the Chicago Gift Show, a guy named Brooks Titcomb whose family owned Woodbury Pewter. Guy had been friends with Brooks and his brother Gordon from playing music together and I got to know Brooks from doing trade shows near his booth. He told me about his potter friend Guy Wolff. Maybe another couple of years later — I had met Brooks in '84 or '85 — Guy had gotten involved with a company based in Kansas called Diamond Brand

Stoneware and they were looking to do a line of reproduction early American style pottery and had come across Guy and thought he might be a good person to design it and head it up." Wolff did do some consulting for them and helped them with some designs but the relationship was brief. "So anyway they had come out onto the market with some of their initial pieces and Guy was out at the Chicago Gift show, must have been the summer of '86 or '87, so we got to talking. We are kindred spirits with our love for the old pottery, so we became friends after that.

"I've got another potter friend in his neck of the woods, Todd Piker of Corn-wall Bridge and so I'd been there to visit Todd, my friend there, and also visited Guy and so it was just a collegial friendship up until '96, I believe it was, when Guy called me and said he was in a real bind with Smith and Hawken because they were flooding him with orders and he couldn't keep up."

Jackson began making pots in seventh grade at the Philbrook Art Center in Tulsa, Oklahoma (now the Philbrook Museum of Art). He built a wheel in his basement with his dad and bought an electric kiln with his paper route earnings before going on to Knox College where he earned a degree in Studio Arts. After that he apprenticed in Minnesota with Wayne Branum and then worked as a production potter for two years at Rowe Pottery. Then he started his own business.

"My business, Rockdale Union Stoneware Pottery, was making reproductions of early American stoneware, so he knew I had a whole production operation put together," Jackson says. "At that time I must have had seven or eight potters working for me, about thirty-five people total. This was back in the time when you could actually make a living selling handmade goods made in the U.S. The market for salt-glazed stoneware was drying up at the time, so it was a real gift — the possibility of doing large volume production for Guy's Smith and Hawken line — so we jumped in with both feet right away. I think the initial call from Guy was in maybe early April of '96 and by the beginning of May we had a purchase order from Smith and Hawken for maybe seventy or eighty thousand dollars worth of stuff and before that had gotten a visit from high corporate folks at Smith and Hawken to check us out because they were so certain that the Guy Wolff stuff would fly that they wanted to find someplace that could do that well."

Jackson and his potters made about seven thousand pieces, all hand thrown, in the first thirty days of their arrangement with Wolff. Jackson had three hard-brick salt kilns that he had been using for his stoneware. Wolff's pots were earthenware and fired to a temperature too low to reactivate the salt vapors, so fortunately they would not have to build new kilns.

Smith and Hawken was particularly excited about Wolff's white pots, which he had originally made for one of his neighbors. "In my area here is a woman named Linda Allard who did a clothing line called Ellen Tracy Clothing," Wolff

Estate or Litchfield pot, white clay, hand-drawn crown, 80 pounds, 21 inches by 22 inches, 2012.

says. "She had her brother [an architect who was designing a house for her] go over to Florence and look at all the Andre Palladio houses." His design for her Connecticut home was built of cut lime-stone in the style of Palladio's grand Italian farm-houses. When she commissioned Wolff to make flowerpots for her, he thought that "it just seemed right to try to find a light-colored clay to go with that house. So I started making white pots and then I started rubbing them with minerals to get a particular look and that ended up being very successful." Allard's garden, Highmeadows, features a potager, formal gardens, stone walls, roses, and Wolff's old-world white pots. It is shown during the Garden Conservancy's Open Days program.

Wolff continued to throw pots in his own shop for sale in his own showroom, and for the specialty garden shops that were carrying his work. He would fly to Wisconsin to work with Jackson and his potters: "I would go off and show first Peter and then his guys in Wisconsin what I was hoping they would do . . . I considered myself as head of Guild. I considered Peter, the Master Potter for that shop."

He was grateful that Peter and his skilled potters were now able to make the pots for Smith and Hawken. He understood, though, that individually, some of the potters would rather be in their own studios making art. They did not have his passion for the flowerpot. "So where an art potter at RISD would say, 'How can you make 500 of that . . . simple pot?' for me it is the most exciting thing because it is a skilled hand moving clay from one place to another and you know where the clay is going . . . that's the description of what traditional pottery is; the piece is known before it starts and there's a particular dance that gets the pot to a certain shape and a lot of things can happen along the way. I remember trying to explain that to the very nice art trained potters who worked in Wisconsin [who came from] the American art school world who then, because they can't make enough money [selling their art pottery] are having to make flowerpots and they are thinking it's not the nicest thing in the world to have to do."

Wolff would explain to them his ideas on how and why a particular shape came into being, telling the young potters, "You have to start with the arch from the beginning and bring it all the way up to the top and then breathe the doming into it and finish on the arch. If you do it that way, it will always come out the same." But this was not what their background had prepared them for and he says, "They would sort of put me aside and say, 'Well, I will get the shape,' but they didn't understand that the way you get the shape is from the method of getting there. I'm not being fussy. I'm being accurate."

Jackson, who possessed the managerial skills that Wolff knew he lacked, kept the pottery moving. He and his potters threw thousands of Wolff's flowerpots for Smith and Hawken, and of course, true to Wolff's beliefs about potting, the more they threw, the better the pots.

Wolff continued to look at old pots. He received invitations to see collections in museums and shards from excavations. Smith and Hawken brought him to the Philadelphia Flower Show

Regency decorated hothouse pot, redware, 2 pounds, 2012.

and while there he went to visit John Bartram's Garden to look at that esteemed collection. John Bartram (1699–1777), the father of American horticulture, and later his descendants beginning with his son William Bartram (1739–1823), filled their extensive Philadelphia garden with plants they collected up and down the east coast or that were sent to them from afar. The garden has been restored and preserved and is now open to the public.

"Finding that collection was a huge deal for me because there were a hundred years of flowerpots from one of *the* most prestigious plant guys who had plants sent to him from all over the world. There were English mixed in with pots probably made in Philly mixed in with I don't know what, so there's a wonderful, wonderful collection of pots there."

Jackson's pottery began to experience financial stress. "We continued to make for Smith and Hawken and some other orders through the rest of '96, maybe some bigger orders, you know in the 20 to 30 thousand dollar range, and we were also working with them on some other projects that did not necessarily relate to Guy Wolff, from little handpainted topiary pots which we weren't able to do, to a square molded pot which we attempted to do but which didn't get ordered by them so at that point, at the end of '96, Rockdale Union Stoneware was in difficult times with our [stoneware] market drying up and our costs going up and up. Rockdale actually filed for Chapter 11 in September of '96. We were trying to reorganize and we were in the process of doing that and we were hopeful that there would be a big Smith and Hawken order in the spring of '97. We really pinned a lot of our hopes on that. We were trying to make a shift from our focus being just strictly early American stoneware to garden pottery inspired by early American pottery and the starting place would be the Guy Wolff line for Smith and Hawken, and expand a line of flowerpots that could be offered to other wholesale customers. We already had probably a thousand wholesale customers who had been buying from us, so we went to the trade shows in January and February showing more of a garden line than our traditional salt glaze line, and got a number of good orders but not nearly enough to sustain us. We kept hoping that we were going to get this big order from Smith and Hawken, and before that could come in, the bank pulled the plug on us and shut us down."

The very day the bank was to foreclose, Jackson received the much-hoped-for hundred thousand dollar purchase order from Smith and Hawken for Guy Wolff pots. He rushed to the bank, and tried to convince his bankers to let them stay in business. With the order from Smith and Hawken, he knew that he could keep Rockdale going. The bankers were not convinced. They refused to give an extension. Rockdale Union Stoneware Pottery was closed.

Now, it was a scramble. Smith and Hawken wanted their order for Guy Wolff pots.

"So with Rockdale being out of the picture, it being liquidated, I started working from my own studio here at home and started in a very small way to do some of the Smith and Hawken work," Jackson says. "They issued some p.o.'s to me, and sort of got built up little by little. It was just me at first, and then I hired a helper I think June of '97. It wasn't another potter, just someone to help with the packing. And then by the fall of '97 I had one or two other potters, at least, working part-time with me, and so we were kind of back into full-scale production, but doing only the Guy Wolff Smith and Hawken line."

But it was too much. They could not keep up. Jackson thought of Holland Millis, who was with Aid to Artisans, which was based out of Connecticut. It was founded in 1976 by James and Mary Plaut to help artisans in third-world countries become self-supporting. James Plaut was the former Secretary General for the World Craft Council. "Holland had a pottery shop going in Honduras. Holland is a former Peace Corps volunteer from the sixties and had spent a lot of time in Africa, Ghana and Kenya, and then had, I think, maybe done a project with Aid To Artisans in Honduras and liked it a lot there. Then he decided he'd like to move there and opened up a workshop." Millis founded Atuto in the early '90s, and Jackson and Millis would see each other every February and August at the New York Gift Show. "Holland knew of my work with Potters for Peace, and we'd always talked about the possibility of me coming to Honduras to work with his potters. I had seen some of the work they were doing and Guy had seen it, and [we] thought these potters have some talents."

Jackson, who speaks Spanish, had been interested in Central America for years and had made numerous trips there since 1989. He was involved with Potters for Peace, an NGO that began as an organization that helped U.S. potters reach out to Nicaraguan potters during the Sandinista-Contra Wars. "The ceramic water filter became the focus for Potters for Peace over the last ten years. Originally the focus was sort of solidarity with potters in Nicaragua, some of them were in communities that were under attack during the Contra War. So initially it was person-to-person solidarity between potters to help out and stand in the way of that war. The ceramic water filter technology started to be wider known in the late nineties and Ron Rivera, who was our Potters for Peace director in Nicaragua, really took it on as his personal crusade to make water filters because he was really into appropriate technology to build workshops to employ people to use tools and raw materials they could find locally. Very tragically, Ron died from malaria contracted during a trip to Nigeria with a team from Princeton University, setting up a water filter workshop. Malaria has an incubation period of about two weeks, so when Ron developed symptoms after his return to Nicaragua, they initially thought it was dengue fever. As Ron's condition deteriorated, they found it was in fact an African strain of malaria. In order to treat it, it requires drugs that were not available in Nicaragua." Readers of *Ceramics Monthly* know the small Potters for Peace ads in the back of the magazine even if they didn't answer the call. "So to head down to Honduras wasn't a big stretch for me but Guy describes it as I dragged him kicking and screaming."

The trip was planned for November 1998 but Hurricane Mitch, one of the deadliest Atlantic storms in history, slammed into Central America at the end of October, leaving 19,000 dead and close to 2.7 million homeless. Honduras, the least developed country in Latin America and the Caribbean at the time, was especially hard hit with mudslides and floods. Honduran homes, farms, roads, hospitals, and infrastructure were severely damaged or buried beneath mud. The media focused the world's attention on the aftermath but aid was slow in coming.

When Wolff and Jackson arrived a month later than planned, they were both stunned by the extensive damage from Mitch. Millis's workshop was in Sabanagrande, a village left back in time, with stone streets and tile roofs and a largely impoverished populace. Jackson says, "Holland, who ran the Sabanagrande workshop, had been a pillar of the community, getting aid out to the people who needed it. He'd always had a focus on his business work there, always trying to figure out of course how to make a profit but how to do it in a way that would help people get a leg up. In Sabanagrande that pottery shop was one of the only places where people could go with some sort of an artisan's skill and earn a living wage. Most people in the town and outside the town were doing subsistence agriculture. There really weren't any other places to earn a wage."

For Wolff, working with the young men at Holland Millis's shop was very different from working with the university-trained potters in Wisconsin. He discovered that the young men in the pottery "had been stonemasons, they'd been digging ditches, they knew that when you spend the whole day using a scythe, you have to hold your arm in a certain way or you will really hurt yourself. So they fussed at me and really took it seriously and that's why that shop is so wonderful. They trusted me. Those guys recognized that I wasn't just giving them an off-handed *do it this way*. Nothing like that. It's the passion of why." In Honduras he worked with people whose own culture was still close to the old ways that he had so admired in Wales and Jugtown. They understood economy of motion and repetition, and what could come from that.

Jackson describes the Honduras experience with similar affection. "When we first got there, there were probably five or six potters, maybe five, and they were all working on kick wheels. Most of them had up to that point been making pottery for maybe two years, two years tops, because they were all pretty young guys, in their late teens, early twenties, and had come to work at Atuto, Holland's business, and so had been trained from scratch in throwing and doing other clay work.

"They were fairly fluent at making straightforward shapes on the wheel. It was an interesting dynamic because none of them had any kind of art school training or anything like that so to work with them was nice. There weren't any pretensions, 'Oh but I'm an artist, I don't do what you want me to do, I only make what I want to make.' They looked at it much more in the traditional artisan manner — [the way] that artisan craftsmen from the nineteenth century, actually what Guy would call preindustrial time — would have looked at it. You trained in this artisan skill to make a product that is useful and hopefully you can make it in a way that is also beautiful.

"And so Guy was sort of in hog heaven with having a group of potters who were almost like clay to be molded, to make things in the way that he wanted them to be made, and with the attitude that he wanted them to be made with rather than — you know, when he had come to train the potters at Rockdale there was a lot of rolling of eyes at him wanting them to make things the way he did, and talking about things the way he did. There was a little of that in Honduras too. Guy can be very dramatic in the way he describes things. I remember at one point Guy sort of leaping around the shop telling people how he wanted this pot to have the arcs that you'd find in a beautiful European cathedral but it should also have the grace of a ballerina, you know all these metaphors, and I have to translate into Spanish, and the potter just looks back at me and says, ask him how tall he wants it."

But Wolff and Jackson agree, the potters in Millis's Sabanagrande shop, Atuto, got it. They understood Wolff. Coming from a culture of handwork, they were sympathetic to his throwing methods. They did good work.

In the beginning the pottery was equipped only with kickwheels and simple updraft kilns. Most potters in Central America still used kilns that were essentially slightly improved pit kilns; more or less permanent cylindrical walls made of mud bricks that were tumble stacked with the wares and fired with brush. These kilns produced pots that were good for cooking or for water jugs, but because the kilns fired unevenly and to only low temperatures, they gave unreliable results. Pots fired in this type of kiln in Mexico gave Latin American pottery a bad reputation in the U.S.

Millis used propane. His burners were rudimentary. The pots were stacked without shelves, which worked fine for flowerpots, as they were stacked one inside another much as had been done in the old country potteries in England. As long as the pots are thrown well, and strong enough to withstand the weight of the pots above them without being crushed, this type of stacking is more efficient than stacking with shelves. But there were cold spots to deal with, and "there would be a pretty good variation, so there were some pots that were really well fired and hard and durable and there were others that were still pretty soft and would chip easily and maybe delaminate when they got wet," Jackson says.

"We got to be friends with everybody there," Jackson continues talking about his and Wolff's relationship with the Honduran potters. "We wanted to help them become more efficient and profitable and we also wanted to be able to get higher output because that's where the demand was and so with some convincing I got Holland to invest in electric wheels for the potters instead of kick wheels. He was dead set against it . . . Holland could be sort of a curmudgeon and stubborn and hard to convince that the way things are might be the way things are." Millis had his own ideas about the best way to make pots, and one of those ideas was that the kickwheel was to be preferred.

One of the best potters was having knee problems, which made kicking painful and difficult and slowed his production, so Millis agreed that he could be given an electric wheel as a trial. "All of a sudden his production was up, thirty, forty per cent over what he had ever been able to do on his best times at the kick wheel. The funny thing was that the other potters saw the way things worked out," and suddenly they all developed knee problems and said to Millis, "'you know what, my knee is hurting too, I need an electric wheel.'" So, the shop was outfitted with electric wheels and everyone's production went up, which made the potters happy as they were paid by the piece.

Glazed pots that touch during a firing, will become stuck fast to each other when the glaze melts and then cools, so stacking the way they did, plus the uneven temperatures, which would make glaze results unpredictable, meant there was no possibility of using glaze in Millis's pottery. Millis developed other ways of giving the pots from his kilns a patina.

"So after they were fired, the pots were given a cold finish," Jackson says. "Holland was a real expert at the different effects you could get just using latex house paint on clay and even doing at the end a thin wash of a certain color and then another color over it and scrubbing it with a Scotch Brite pad or with sandpaper or something like that. There was a lot of handwork that went into the finishes . . . and they looked really great . . . In fact we came up with one finish that was just for Smith and Hawken that they absolutely loved . . . we called it a moss finish but it didn't really look like a moss finish, but looked like it had been weathered, that maybe it had been painted at one point but it had weathered. It looked as old as the hills." Smith and Hawken wanted an exclusive on the moss pots and "began buying 40-foot container load after 40-foot container load of Guy Wolff pots made in Honduras."

Just prior to this, Wolff and Jackson began to think about making pots for the small retail shops that had been Jackson's customers. In January of 1999, after working with the Honduran potters, they had the new pots shipped directly to the gift show in Atlanta where they wrote orders totaling more than $150,000.

Smith and Hawken offered other pots besides Guy Wolff pots. One line from Portugal was not selling well. Wolff says, "The throwing was beautiful. The pots were just stupid. They were a bad idea." He offered to go to Portugal and work with the potters, and said, "I want to go to your shop and train them to make pots for you. So Peter being the person who had the money, paid for us to get on the plane." The folks at Smith and Hawken did not quite understand what he meant, as he was not going to train them to make his pots but they were happy to let Wolff try to work with them.

"Guy always had a fantasy about trying to work in England with English potters and doing more traditional higher-fired, frost-proof English terracotta," Jackson says. So the trip (in 2002) began with the two of them traveling around England. In England they visited potters and potteries that Wolff knew and looked at pots. Then they went to visit the Portuguese potters doing work for Smith and Hawken.

Potters had been making pots in this village for seven or eight hundred years. It was here that Wolff saw the hinged wooden pot lifters that go inside a pot, making it possible to remove a good sized pot directly from the wheel head without throwing on a bat. He says he remembers leaning over to Jackson and saying, "That's made the whole trip worthwhile."

He watched the potters and told them, "'Remember what your great-grandfather made,' and they just shrugged their shoulders and said, 'You have to be kidding, don't you want us to make this or this?' And I said, 'No, I want you to make good Mediterranean historical urns with a little bit of glaze around the top, of a type that would have been made here 200 years ago." They knew the old shapes, the shapes that were indigenous to their village, and once they began making them again, their pots had beauty and vigor.

"Every shop has always had that one special eye that's good. So in Honduras there was this one guy whose father was a stonemason and he just had this impeccable eye. An eye isn't something you can train. You either have it or you don't . . . I would say, show me the shop and I will tell you what we can do with it. Because you have to start from the material, and you have to start from the people, and from the history of the place and make something honest that resonates with the spot. If you don't do that, things will not be beautiful. So that's been a brick wall in the industrial world because it is very hard to pull off. It was easiest when I was working with Peter. His wish to accommodate the market and my wish to keep to my design precepts made for an interesting and honest tension between us.

"Before Peter Jackson, the day that I got my first computer, I sent an email to the two women [Mara Seibert and Lenore Rice from Seibert and Rice] who import pots from [Impruneta] Florence and said I really love your pots. If I ever do a book, I would love to talk about who you are and what you do."

"He came to us probably in '98," Mara Seibert says, echoing his account. "And told us if he were ever to do a book, he would want to do a chapter on Seibert and Rice, and we started corresponding. His daughter was very ill at that time and he got a computer to research her illness and in doing so he also Googled flowerpots and we came up."

Mara Seibert and Lenore Rice had founded Seibert and Rice almost by accident four years prior. Seibert had been in corporate finance with J.P. Morgan Chase and Rice had been a tax attorney for Sherman Sterling. Both women had left their high-powered positions to stay home with young children, and lived in the same town but did not know each other. A mutual friend rented a home in Tuscany and invited the two women and their families to share it. "Lenore knew a lot about Tuscany. She's very knowledgeable and she speaks fluent Italian and she said one day, 'Oh there's this town that's famous for making the most beautiful terracotta in the world, over the hill. Do you want to go?' So we went. And we were just bowled over. We had never seen such beautiful artistry. Such beautiful color. There was nothing like it in the United States."

Impruneta, a pretty town in the old pinewood hills of Tuscany, outside Florence, has been home to potters at least since the eleventh century when local artisans made floor and roof tiles. By the early fourteenth century pottery had become the primary industry and in addition to tiles, many domestic wares were produced. The kilns flourished during the Renaissance. By the early seventeenth century, large oil jars, urns and flowerpots were being made and are to this day.

Seibert and Rice fell in love with the soft rosy hues of the pots, the wonderful shapes, the sizes, some simple, some intricately ornate and all of it made by hand. "We walked around with the owner, one of three brothers, and we said we want to buy pots for each of our homes. He didn't want to sell to us because we were two housewives!" Seibert continues. "And so we go back to the house and we call a customs broker, a freight forwarder, we buy lira. We went back to him the next day and said, 'The truck is coming to pick up our goods next week.' And he said, 'OK' . . . So I wrote the guy a check and he said, 'Oh it will be there in a month,' and then I thought I will never see the money and I will never see the pots. And a month comes and a truck pulls up to my house [in New Jersey] and we unloaded the pallets and we unpacked them and I said these are just gorgeous . . . Well in the meantime, Lenore and I were both thinking about going back to work, but in different capacities. We couldn't be putting in the 80-hour weeks that we had been putting in for a decade with small children. She had just passed her New Jersey bar. I was looking to buy a little company. So we put a little budget together and a little catalog. We literally put some pieces in Lenore's station wagon and we went to high-end interior decorators and floral shops in Manhattan and the suburbs and everyone placed orders, and so we began." The following year, they won best in show at the New York Flower Show.

Wolff was thrilled to discover that there were flowerpots "on the market that were completely handmade . . . so we started this dialogue and then it really turned into a situation with him designing flowerpots for us for our line."

"It was just amazing," Wolff says. "So I made some little pots of the shapes that I wanted. I did a line of about five pieces that would do different jobs in the garden and of all the import stuff that I've done, I'm most proud of this grouping from Impruneta."

"I did not go to Italy. The potters are so good, I did not need to. I sent some prototypes by plane. I didn't have to teach anybody anything. I just had to say, make something beautiful. So big pots from Florence happened first. That was the first interaction of that sort. That project is still chugging along. Those five pots are still selling internationally."

"There are several things that are special about Impruneta terracotta," Seibert says. "One is the soil. The soil has a very high iron and calcium content. And the pots are high-fired." The remarkable consequence of the unusual clay and the high temperature fires is that earthenware made in Impruneta is frostproof to minus 20°F. Horticultural pots can be left outside in areas with snowy subzero winters, not just California or around the Mediterranean. Even the largest oil jars and flowerpots made in Impruneta can continue to serve as focal points in the northern landscape in January, relieving the gardener of the task of lugging heavy pots to a storage shed. The other consequence is the color.

"It's funny," Seibert says, "because Greve in Chianti is only a fifteen-minute drive. Their soil produces great wine and in Impruneta the soil is so drastically different they don't grow good grapes. But they make beautiful terracotta. And it is the only terracotta in the world that is truly frostproof because of the soil and the firing process. You know most other pots are only fired for a day or two and they never reach that high firing process. They go in and they fire up to 2,000 and they cool down for the next couple of days. And the soil is a dark gray color and then it turns this beautiful pink color, you know a very rosy color when it comes out . . . When we first started the business it was just cheap orange terracotta pots here in the states and then a lot of these manufacturers caught on and now they are adding chemicals to their terracotta to give it the soft color and not the hard edge to it.

"During the Renaissance," Seibert continues, "a lot of artists from Florence went to Impruneta to work with this beautiful clay, like della Robbia and others, and that resulted in the family workshops. There is one workshop that we deal with whose building dates from the early sixteen hundreds. And it's generational . . . handed off to the next generation, and it takes quite a while for someone to become skilled. Typically an apprentice's pots will be thrown out for a year until the master feels they have accomplished the technique."

Seibert and Rice formed relationships with several terracotta workshops, each of which had been making pots for generations. All the pots are individually handmade. There are three methods: pots can be thrown on a wheel, they can be pressed into a mold, or they can be built up with coils. Pots pressed into molds and pots that are coiled can be very large, much larger than possible to make on a wheel. The press-molded pots can also be very ornate. Some molds have been in use for generations.

"One workshop that is a one-man operation," Seibert says, is run by "a true sculptor, so we give him the very detailed ones [in their catalog such as the] Chanteloop that Charlotte Moss designed that is very, very detailed. We had him make the Abbie Zabor Critter Vase, which is totally handthrown and the Gertrude pot [designed by] Guy Wolff, that is completely thrown on a wheel and then he emblazes the rim with a little texture. Guy's Conservatory Planter is also handthrown.

"Then we have another workshop in Impruneta that does slightly more rustic work where this first one is a little more refined." Wolff's Hampton Pot is made here in press molds: "The Hampton pot doesn't have a rim so when it dries and fires it gets a little wobbly, and it really looks good, and while they are handmade in molds they look thrown. The Peale Pot — when that comes out of the mold, they have to fine-tune things with tools. That rim is a very delicate rim and that one gets kind of a nice wobble to it. They are press molded . . . they pound the clay into [the mold], and then it dries for a while and they take pieces off and they touch up the pot."

Press molding is as much handwork as throwing on the wheel, and takes years of practice and great skill. In his own shop, Wolff throws the Peale Pot and uses one of his homemade coggles for the famous rim. He also throws the Hampton. He does use press molds that he has made, for the plates that he covers with slip and joggles, much as most earthenware plates in early America were press molded. But because press molding allows for intricate three-dimensional design, it is used for the Peales in Impruneta.

Most of the kilns are gas fueled. "One is still wood burning," Seibert says. "There's one that's a two million dollar high tech kiln . . . The one that makes three pots for Guy is in an old kiln within a kiln. He put his gas kiln into one of these domed rooms; they brick up the wall, similar to a bottle kiln, so he has his gas kiln in that space. Most of them have converted. The one that has the wood burning also has a pretty high tech kiln but they use both. It's a fascinating process. Each pot takes about a month to make. They make the pot, have it dry, and then the firing process."

Wolff explains in an early catalog, "I am so excited and happy to have the chance to do this project with Lenore and Mara of Seibert & Rice. The work they have brought over from Impruneta has always been a joy for me to see, and I am very proud to be invited to work with them and their potters."

He goes on to describe the five pots in the catalog, two of which, the Peale Pot and the Hartford Pot, are deeply associated with all of his work. "The Conservatory Pot [19 inches wide by 10 inches tall] was inspired by my visit to the Enid Haupt Conservatory just after it was restored . . . The Gertrude Pot [17.5 inches wide by 19 inches tall] is inspired by Gertrude Jekyll's gardening and her love for the Greek line and it is dedicated to her. I have put together the simplest of classic lines on a colonnade base and added a little art deco decoration to the rim . . . The Hampton Pot [20 inches wide by 13.5 inches tall] was inspired by the beautiful gardens I was lucky enough to see on Long Island, New York . . . The Peale Pot [20 inches wide by 18.5 inches tall] is inspired by the portrait *Rubens Peale with Geranium* . . . The Hartford Pot [22.5 inches wide by 16 inches tall] was derived from pieces found in Hartford, Connecticut, and Salem, Massachusetts, in the nineteenth century . . ." As I write this in 2012, these pots are featured prominently in Seibert and Rice's online catalog.

Wolff and Seibert and Rice are concerned about the future, as, after all these many hundreds of years, and multiple generations of making pots using methods passed down from parent to child, the younger Imprunetians are losing interest. "Guy and I were just talking about this recently, we've been doing this for about 20 years and the families are in their mid to late fifties, sixties and none of their children want to go into the trade. This is the first time we are seeing a dying art. We have one workshop that has three brothers and I would say they are all fifty-five plus. They have eight to ten kids between the three brothers and only one son is going into the business. And then the one that does the very fine work, the one-man workshop, has two twins in their early twenties and neither the boy nor the girl wants to go into it. And then the third workshop that makes three of the garden pots has two daughters and they have no interest in going into the business. So we've talking how could we sponsor something, it's just early on in the thinking, maybe getting together with some of these workshops and finding out whether there's an art school in Florence that could send students to Impruneta for the summer to learn how. This has never happened before."

"As far as the theory of that thing, the thing that happened in Impruneta and the thing that happened in Portugal, that was taking shops that were wonderful, shops that you thought were just great . . . and you get to support them by asking them to make something that was true to their own history. That's very easy to pull off and if the storytelling on it is done well, the American garden comes along for the ride.

"White Flower Farm has very cleverly gone and gotten the beautiful pots from Crete. You know they just get containers of these very beautiful pots and it's a done deal. They were wonderful a thousand years ago, two thousand years ago and they are wonderful today. So you take an oil urn and fill it up with some flowers. Some of this isn't even designing. It's just finding something wonderful and then saying this is something the world should see. I get very confused when people say, 'oh you are a designer when you go overseas.' I will say, 'I am a person who makes pots who is a fan of people who make beautiful pottery.' The only reason my name is on the pot is to say, I think this is a beautiful thing. There's a side of what you would call design work for a larger market that is connected back to trying to make sure that the handcraft that we are all excited about is given a chance and nurtured."

Wolff and Jackson were asked to consult for a company that was making garden pots in Malaysia for the mass market. They were dismayed to find that the potters had lost their throwing tradition, but pleased to discover that they had kept some of their traditional shapes. They visited a Mr. Yap, whose pots were all jigger jolleyed, but beautiful. Wolff was astonished at Yap's output. Nothing came of that trip, though, except some photos to bring home.

Jackson met the owners of Napa Home and Garden at the Atlanta Gift Show and got to know them. They were already making and selling garden pots and liked Wolff's work. "And so we started talking about developing what we called the Guy Wolff Greenhouse line that could be specifically for Napa to market to their much bigger customer base," Jackson says. "Guy's idea on it was that these should echo the pots that were made during Victorian times to supply estate garden conservatories." Napa Home and Garden was already working with potters in Vietnam. So Wolff and Jackson went to Vietnam. Jackson continues, "That trip to Vietnam was to work with a pottery that I had found out about there that could do hand throwing and antique terracotta finishes. So we jumped in there and had initially very good results." Napa paid them a royalty for their work.

However, tensions arose. Jackson explains, "Napa was moving more of their production to China instead of Vietnam and wanted to consolidate so they could ship more efficiently. So I went to China for Napa to try to develop an existing pottery shop that could make Guy's shapes and do it handthrown in a way that would meet the quality that Guy expected and that our customers wanted [later Wolff also went to work with the potters]. So that initially worked pretty well although there's never been a very strong connection between the owners of Napa and Guy. They come at it from completely different ends of the spectrum. Guy's all about form and function and aesthetics and Napa was all about getting it made at the lowest possible cost so they could sell it at the lowest possible price and do a high volume of it, and so, really without even consulting Guy, they moved some of the production into being jiggered instead of hand thrown and Guy didn't find out about it until later on and he was pretty pissed about it [and it was discontinued and throwing reinstated]. So with Napa there have been a lot of bumps in the road in trying to make the Guy Wolff line hit its full potential. Since Guy and K. C. Cunningham [owner of Napa Home and Garden] just weren't on the same wavelength about a lot of things, so there wasn't much synergy in them working together. I was trying to be the go-between for that, and to a certain extent was successful in helping to develop the Guy Wolff line for Napa but the pots were never quite as good aesthetically as they were when Guy and I were working together and I had my own company.

"There's one factory in China that makes Guy Wolff pots, actually there are two different ones, there's one that makes the pots descended from the ones that we were making in Honduras, a little bit different, but essentially the same line, called the Guy Wolff Guild Pots and the Guy Wolff Green House Pots. And then another factory, Guy and I made a trip there I think in November of '09, specifically to work on a line for Restoration Hardware and, sort of ancillary to that, was developing some new pieces for Napa. Actually they just took a line that is partially glazed and partially cold finished. "The Restoration Hardware adventure was a big new chapter at one point although it didn't last as long as we had hoped it would. When Smith and Hawken went under in July of 2009, one of the buyers that I had worked with for years at Smith and Hawken ended up landing at Restoration Hardware. They are all sort of in the same neighborhood in Marin County outside of San Francisco. And so Restoration Hardware and probably some other companies too were looking to see how they could fill up the vacuum that had been left behind in the garden world. And so they asked us to make a presentation and we ended up doing a Guy Wolff line specifically for them. They were rolling out a whole new garden line and so we were in with them in a big way, developing a full line in 2010. Unfortunately they decided to switch directions [because] their customers weren't really into gardening, they were more into décor. So the kind of gardening items they now carry are more like large outdoor containers. We did a full line of pretty interesting pieces for them we called the Regency Collection that were done in the white clay we had originally done for Smith and Hawken and some were done in a gray clay that we'd developed specifically for Restoration Hardware. But they decided for 2011 to not continue that line and really started slowing down what they did in gardening in general. The last Guy Wolff pots [for Restoration Hardware] were for holiday 2011. We developed a line of Guy Wolff bulb pots and herb kits for them, and they sold them very well but they, Restoration Hardware, continued to go in a different direction. Upscale furniture and home décor have a higher sales dollar per square foot than garden pottery."

Today, the Guy Wolff pots for Napa Home & Garden are sold primarily through brick-and-mortar shops, though there are online sales too. They are handthrown at a family-owned and operated pottery in Chaozhou, a city in East Guangdong province of the People's Republic of China. Chaozhou, which looks out on the South China Sea, is bisected by two rivers, the Hanjiang and Huanggang and blessed with rich clay deposits. The city's ceramic tradition goes back at least a thousand years, with a cluster of kilns near the Han River dating back to the Tang Dynasty and later the Song dynasty. During the Song period it was known as One Hundred Kiln Village. Potters in Chaozhou produced Chinese export porcelain, which was in high demand throughout the western world.

The city government describes the town as "cradleland of ceramic culture" and the "city of ceramics."[1] There are humble little shops run by potters working in their backyards and there are huge computerized ceramic factories six stories tall and four to six blocks long. They make everything from handthrown pieces to sanitary ware to electronic porcelain insulators. The shop that throws the Wolff pots is run by a husband and wife and their kids and employs about two hundred people.

"Five years ago Chaozhou was a city of 10 million people with 15,000 pottery factories," Jackson says. "You've got a huge industry supporting all that. You can find any kind of glaze you want within a mile radius of where you are working. To find a certain red to match a Pantone color you might search high and low in the states; in Chaozhou, you can find it in the neighborhood." Traditionally, potters in the city were famous for their green glaze but produced many colors.

Wolff demonstrating in Yixing, China, where potters have worked for more than a thousand years. Peter Wakefield Jackson says, "This factory was one that Guy and I liked very much. The owner, Mowah Yong, was born, raised and went to art school in Holland. His grandfather had been Chinese, and he emigrated to China 20 or more years ago and ended up marrying a woman whose family had always been in the pottery business. He was a kindred spirit to me and Guy, with an eye for good pots, and an appreciation and understanding of a more European aesthetic." Photo courtesy of Peter Wakefield Jackson

While in Chaozhou, Wolff saw the great dragon kilns, and was deeply impressed watching a potter build a huge jar entirely with coils. "While we were in Shanghai we went to the museum and we spent four or five hours looking at the beautiful vases and then, for whatever reason, we walked downstairs and we went into the room with all the bronze and it just hit me like a ton of bricks,

Empire pot with "G. Wolff Pottery, Bantam, CT." coggled around the rim, white clay, 6 pounds, 2012.

they were so beautiful." The fact that ceramic shapes were made and then the molten bronze was poured into these clay vessels to make the bronzes was "just magic" to him.

He had admired Asian pottery since he was young and, as with the early American and English pots, had thought about what made the pots good. "I love Han and Tang Dynasty pottery a lot, I love the Korean celadons, the looseness, the informal formality, amused, playful things that the Koreans did. And I love the formal uprightness of the Japanese throwing. They have a sense of compression that is unlike anyone else's in the world. I have a sort of very developed picture if someone were to say Japanese pottery to me; right away I would see that compressed line, those Tamba pieces. A jar from Japan is just tighter and more controlled almost past the point of being able to bear it. The clay is so organized.

Whereas the best of the Chinese pots are so balanced as to be almost invisible. That's really important to me. When I think of the best pots from the Sung Dynasty, they are almost invisible. There ... isn't an influence, it's just completely and utterly of itself. That's why certain sorts of what might be called Chinese peasant pots are so invisible because they are so balanced. The Korean joy is the opposite of the Chinese and Japanese both. It's so in love with the material that they let the material do it. You could say they are so in love with the material and in love with the play. The great Korean pottery has the same playfulness that an otter does jumping through the water. It's impossible to do. I don't know how it happens. So being loose and playful in that moment isn't easy."

With his Guilds, Wolff has found an interesting way to make more pots than he could alone in his own shop. It has not been easy. There have been challenges. He says he has been "married to Peter" in this — not in a personal way, he has a wife and family — but in the way married partners often work together. Peter now works fulltime for Napa Home & Garden, but keeps Wakefield Studio going at his home in Wisconsin, making his own pots when he is not at his day job.

Wolff has insisted the Guild pots be handmade, formed by potters' palms and fingers rather than the cold metal of machines. He has been able to help potters in distant parts of the world, many with long ceramic traditions behind them, reconnect with their clay heritage and let their hands move the material in the way that it wants to be moved for each particular shape. And with the Guild work, he has been able to bring beautiful handmade flowerpots into the gardens and onto the windowsills of people who might not otherwise have known anything other than industrially made planters.

Along with this have come more demands on his time to leave his shop and throw pots for an audience. "The thing that I find very exciting with a little bit of celebrity is to be able to do something helpful for the world," he says. "So here we are making these pots all over the world, and garden shops are selling this less expensive line, what we call G. Wolff and Co., and I will go out and make pots at a place like Chicago or Santa Fe or a place like Naples, Florida, a place that maybe there is a family that has two or three garden stores, and they have me come down. Now that costs them a lot of money to have me come, because I have to close my shop, so how can we turn this into something bigger than that? How can we turn it into something that is fun, and more meaningful than just here is somebody who is a little known for making flowerpots. My daughter had an illness, my wife had an illness, all centered around cancer, so I will go to a place like Naples, Florida, and will do two days of throwing, maybe two thousand dollars worth of pots made, that are then auctioned off for Susan Komen. It is meaningful for a number of reasons. Sometimes somebody who has had a family member who has passed will ask me to write their name on a pot and the dates or some special saying that will mean something, and you can have this powerful interaction with human beings, and then there's also flowerpots being sold. It doesn't have to be just about the flowerpots. I remember there was one [demonstration] in San Diego where the children's chemo ward [benefited]. It was very, very meaningful . . . It can be for the Hole in the Wall Camp here in Connecticut or Prairie Kids in Chicago or Komen. It makes it so that when I am getting on an airplane to go do this, they may be paying me, but I feel like there is something bigger than just a visit from some semi-known flowerpot maker, something larger and touching more real people."

Recently, Wolff has been stamping his English-inspired pots with a crown.
Here he draws an exuberant crown freehand with a needle pin on a 24-pound pot.

CHAPTER EIGHT

Mud Man, Poet of Flowerpots

"Pretend you know only Guy Wolff's work (as might be of a potter 100 years ago)," Mrs. Karl writes, describing Wolff's pots and how to look at them. *"The evidence is there of some wonderful potter through a recognizable hand (setting those pots above the other good pots of the era). Don't imagine the potter who makes them; just define (for yourself) what it is that these pots have. The potter alone didn't make them. I mean that when a pot is that good, it has a life of its own and it is not necessary to know who made it. Try that and see what the pots tell you."*[1]

Elaborating on what sets Wolff's pots apart, she continues, "The reason (or one main reason) why Guy is not a big name in the current 'art potter' scene is that he is not an 'art potter' and he makes round pots . . . round pots result from wheel action. A non-thrower I know who makes use of a wheel says, 'I throw but then I alter the shapes.' — Well, if a *real* thrower is in action, there is absolutely nothing that you would want to alter. The vitality in Guy's pots is so great because they get there so fast (throwing *should* be fast) and that (in *his* case 'cause he's beyond necessity) whether or not the pot is 'centered' — 'cause he is the *Master* and can bring it all into orbit no matter how 'casual' the getting up there was. The vitality of the form is all in how it got there. 'Oh it's not even — that side goes out more than the other.' But, does it fall down anywhere along the way? NO. Is it still moving after the wheel has stopped? YES!!! He can also make a perfect pot if he wants to and the clay needs 'attention' 'cause it is not so plastic. — In any case — there is no other wheel worker I know of in Guy's category. Perfect poise."

Turning to Wolff's interest in the Mingei movement, Mrs. Karl continues, "Guy loved Hamada Shoji and he wanted to contribute to what Hamada stood for. At the time (now quite a few years ago) there was a Japanese student [at High Mowing] that we liked very much, Shushi, and she liked us — we had a close connection — my daughter Brigitta tutored her. Shushi was going home to Japan and could and would carry a Wolff pot with her and deliver it directly to the museum. This was a gift that Guy wanted to give."[2]

Wolff was taken with the integrity and beauty of Hamada's pots and interested in how he lived, creating for himself beautiful surroundings. Hamada believed that there was inherent beauty in humble everyday items made anonymously by hand. He liked the English country pottery that he saw when he was in England, and had pieces shipped back to Japan so he could look at them. He and his close friends Söetsu Yánagi and Kanjirö Kawai (1890–1966) visited antique and second-hand shops and roamed the villages collecting preindustrial pieces made of wood, clay, straw, and fabric by artisans in Japan. They saw great beauty in these humble items.

To further a wider appreciation for these folk crafts, Yánagi, Hamada, and Kawai founded the Mingei movement in 1926. "I cannot forget the night in January, 1926, when in company with Kanjirö Kawai and Shöji Hamada at the great mountain monastery of Köya-San we made the decision to start a national collection of folk arts," Yánagi recalled.[3] Ten years later, the Mingeikan

Museum or Japan Folk Crafts Museum opened in Tokyo. Housed in a compound of classical Japanese buildings, one an old building originally intended for Yánagi and brought in from the countryside where Hamada lived, the Museum holds over 17,000 craft objects of various materials including clay, wood, metal, and fiber.

"Almost all the things in the folk craft museum are handmade. The period of handmade goods was extremely long, and during the mere fifty or sixty years of Japanese industrialism it can hardly be expected that the objects produced are very good or beautiful," Yánagi, the first director, wrote of the Museum. "On reflection, one must conclude that in bringing cheap and useful goods to the average household, industrialism has been of service to mankind, — but at a cost of the heart, of warmth, friendliness, and beauty. By contrast, articles well made by hand, though expensive, can be enjoyed in homes for generations, and, this considered, they are not expensive after all."[4]

The men had spent hours together and apart, in solitary contemplation, often while looking at a particular pot, or together deep in discussion, trying to get at what it was that made the folk crafts they were collecting so beautiful. Hamada argued that it was the honesty and quality of the materials, the utility of the objects, and the accessibility to the practice of the crafts.

"If one is observing a pot or any good article," he wrote, "one must be aware that 'taste' is only partial viewing, while perceiving the 'feeling' of an article is seeing the whole . . . The same distinction also applies to the craftsman doing his work; he can consciously create tasteful things but he cannot deliberately create things with feeling. Real feeling seems to hover impartially; it is something inherent in the nature of a work."[5]

Wolff, wishing to pay tribute, and with Mrs. Karl's encouragement, sent a tall, dark Albany-slip-glazed jar that he had originally made for her, to Japan with the student. Mrs. Karl wrote a laudatory and explanatory note (now lost) to go with it. Shushi, the young woman who transported the piece, arrived at the Museum on a day that it was closed. She was told to come back on Saturday, dressed in her traditional kimono, and make her presentation at the special dinner they were holding that night.

Teiko Utsumi, then a trustee and director of the Museum wrote back to Wolff, thanking him:

MINGEIKAN

THE JAPAN FOLK-CRAFTS MUSEUM

4–3–33 KOMABA-KU

TOKYO 153 JAPAN

MAY 12, 2000

DEAR GUY WOLFF,

First of all, it was a great honor to receive your heart warm gift of your precious work. Risaki Koyama brought personally to the Nihon Mingeikan on Saturday April 8, 2000.

What a nice form and shape with iron glaze with the history which was explained by Mrs. Karl of High Mowing School! The reason I asked Risaki to visit me on that evening of April 8, was that there was a big party at the Nihon Mingeikan. We hold such a function in every two years or so. There I thought I could show it to the important people of the museum who were gathering that evening. I showed it to Mr. Sori Yanagi who is the first son of Mr. Soetsu Yanagi, Dr. H. Mizuo who was the president of Musashino Art University and many more.

Surely, your work became part of the museum collection together with explanation of important relation of Soetsu Yanagi, Shoji Hamada and YOU.

I must apologize that I took so long to express our deep appreciation to you until today. Our museum publishes a monthly magazine entitled MINGEI. In the next issue, with your permission, I would like very much to translate part of your letter and write about you, together with a photograph of your vase you gave to us.

I wish you best of luck for your future work in good health and spirit. Thank you again very much for your gift.

VERY SINCERELY YOURS,

TEIKO UTSUMI

Trustee

International Programs Director

Utsumi did publish a piece about his vase and remained an admirer. Wolff kept in touch with her and tried to generate interest in and support for the museum in the U.S. Ironically or, as Wolff thinks, fittingly, there is no longer a trace of the vase he sent. It has, Wolff says, become "unknown." What better tribute to the Mingei movement than that?

Wolff attends a few large shows and symposium such as the annual symposium at North Hill, in Vermont. "A big show for New England is called Trade Secrets, which is one Bunny Williams does . . . The way I would describe that to people is, if you want to see what Martha or the de la Rentas are going to put in their garden this year, come out and see what they are doing . . . There's sort of a social side to gardening. I have a friend who is in the racehorse business and it is pretty related. There's a high end to gardening that is a lot of fun. I have never been to the Chelsea Flower Show. I've never had the money to go to that one. But it is amazing what you see happen in Philadelphia. Bulldozers come in. And they put piles of dirt and they build hillsides. I think one year Venice was the theme so there was a gondola. So there are different levels of what you might call the garden club. There's the Pennsylvania Horticultural Society [producers of the Philadelphia International Flower Show] down to the rudest garden club. They're both a lot of fun."

Wolff's pots have continued to be featured in magazine pieces about gardens, such as a 1997 piece by Sarah Gray Miller called *High Style, Down to Earth* on Linda Allard's garden in *Garden Design.* In May of 2002, *Garden Magazine* did a piece on Wolff called "Pots With a Past," with photos by Rob Cardillo. In addition to photos of his pots overflowing with plants, the magazine had Wolff pose as if he were Rubens Peale, and featured the photo next to the painting that meant so much to him. He thought it was silly but went along with it. In April 2005, *Early American Life* featured Tamulevich's piece "American Flowerpots," which included photos of Wolff's pots at the Stonington, Connecticut, Historical Society's "A Place to Take Root" exhibit, which she curated. Tamulevich embarked on what was planned to be a three-year tour of the exhibit, but which has continued beyond that time. She has asked each host location to contribute information about their region's early flowerpots, with the object of creating an index of traditional American flowerpots, and one hopes, perhaps the definitive book on the topic. Wolff continues to be engaged with the project.

He appeared on a total of nine Martha Stewart shows. After her first televised visit to his shop, he did shows with her in her Westport, Connecticut, studio on repairing pots and planting amaryllis, shows delivering pots to her Westport garden and planting at her house, a show on the white flowerpots, and another on vases filmed at his Woodville shop, one on flower arranging, and a last show with his son Ben Wolff. He also worked on or suggested a few other segments for her.

In 2006 and 2007 Wolff made a new workshop and moved from the old

Redware
pitchers, pans,
and flowerpots
displayed in a
rustic cupboard in
Wolff's shop.

barn in Woodville to an antique two-room house built around 1735, just three minutes up the road. The shingled house was in frightening disrepair but had beautiful lines. Originally, he and his wife Erica Warnock thought they would restore the little house to live in, but that would have been prohibitively expensive, plus it was too close to the road for comfort. They decided to build a house farther back on the property and convert the little house into a new workshop.

Wolff tore off the early-twentieth-century addition and stripped the house down to the heavy wood frame, saving the oak plank siding. Rebuilt, the plank siding back in place, this would become his showroom. The attic would be a place for his collection of pots and his books. A saltbox addition was built across the back on a cement slab for a 16 by 33 foot workspace. The slab extends beyond the shop, to an open-air workspace for drying pots. Here there is a farm-type outdoor faucet, which is his water supply.

The new exterior siding was painted the red of so many New England farmhouses but the doors were left to silver. The front door faces a flat gravel area with cement block and board shelves for displaying pots. A side door opens to the drive. Both public entrances are graced with enormous but nicely flat granite stepping-stones. There are several auricula theaters, painted green, set up outside close to the building for the display of pots.

His sign, sometimes just a bit obscured by the forsythia growing along busy Route 202, is out front, with a rhubarb forcer and old wheelbarrow. It's a pretty, efficient studio. Wolff's eye when it comes to display would be the envy of any retailer or gallery owner, with the pots massed, grouped, artfully stacked, and here and there, highlighted. The fixtures are a combination of cupboards built by a local cabinetmaker (there's information to order your own from him), Marcel Breuer's scarred workbench from his garage, a few antiques and built-in shelves made from salvaged wood.

The workshop addition, airy and bright, with paddle fans on the ceiling, can be accessed from the showroom through an interior doorway. Barely more than 500 square feet, it is organized and efficient, and importantly, can be heated in winter, but it is not at all luxurious. Many professional potters are used to far larger quarters.

Partially glazed redware jugs and pitchers displayed in Wolff's shop.

Coggles, ribs, cutting wires, and (on the lower left) Portuguese pot lifters. Many of these tools, made by Wolff, are works of art themselves. He keeps them neatly arranged and ready on the wall behind his wheels.

Most visitors to Guy Wolff Pottery come to buy pots. They learn that when the flag is up, the shop is open. He greets everyone, "Welcome to Guy Wolff Pottery." When the flag is down, he is away or in the house, or something such as a magazine photo shoot is taking place. Route 202 is a busy road. Some of the occupants of the 10,000 cars a day that pass by, stop out of curiosity or because they have always meant to. But most visitors come with intent. They have heard of Guy Wolff or they already have his pots and want more.

The shop is an experience itself. You are taken into Wolff's world and for a half hour or so, leave your own world behind you. You are embraced by the ancient oak walls of the old house and the hundreds of Wolff's distinctive flowerpots that line them, pots in red and white clays touched with minerals. There, too, are his earthenware jugs and jars, his stoneware vases, the joggled and slip-trailed work. Outdoors, you can wander in the gardens, and see his pots, most of them large, lushly planted by his wife, and imagine how your garden will look when you have a few of his pots of your own. And then you see him at work, at his wheel, and he is always ready to talk, to tell you how the pots are made. He is a storyteller, an entertainer, and a teacher. Wolff is the docent. Wolff and his pottery are the exhibit. What you get, in addition to the

handthrown pots you might choose to purchase, is the opportunity to share his way of life for a few moments.

In July of 2006, *Better Homes and Gardens* sent a photo crew to take photos of Wolff's pots in his wife's garden for the summer 2007 issue of *Country Gardens*. Their idea was to feature the garden as much as the pots. This was a problem because Wolff was in the midst of working on the new shop, and he and his wife did not yet have much of a garden when the magazine first called about setting up the shoot. But they had planned to make one to show Wolff's pots in use, a place for visitors to wander, so they enlisted some help, and created an abundant and colorful oasis in time for the magazine staff's arrival.

There are other visitors, those who come to make music with him, and other potters who come from around the world to chat, to learn, to see what Wolff is doing. Simon Leach, grandson of Bernard Leach and son of David Leach, and a famous potter himself, is known for his quietly elegant domestic wares. He says, "The first time I visited him was March of 2009. At the time I was living and working in Spain. I saw Guy working on the wheel on YouTube and I thought he was someone I could learn from so I rang him up and asked, can I come over and spend a few days with you. I took a flight over from Madrid to New York and I spent a few days with Guy in his studio . . . I'm not really a garden pot maker, although I do occasionally make a flowerpot. I am more a domestic potter and I am working at high temperatures, and my work is glazed and it is very different [from Wolff's], but I saw his ability to throw and move clay and I wanted to learn something. I did actually. I learned a few things. You can always learn." Leach has made and posted more than 800 YouTube videos, and made a couple while he was with Wolff. The first is of Wolff throwing a 25-pound flowerpot. Leach says, of Wolff in his video, "It's amazing how he can move the clay like that. You might think to move clay like that you have to be incredibly strong; well, strength has something to do with it, but it's technique that is very important. He had a technique that was slightly different from mine so I thought I should go over there and become his apprentice for a few days, and it did improve my throwing. I should go over again and stretch myself. It's a different thing throwing pots like that than instead of little coffee cups . . . and he's not firing at high temperatures . . . He has a great gift and a lot to give to people. I am glad he puts things out on YouTube about pottery making because I don't know anybody throwing clay like he is on that scale . . . 25-pound flowerpots and it's great work."

Other visitors from the U.K. include Douglas Fitch, a slipware potter who owns Hollyford Pottery in Devonshire, England; and Hannah McAndrew, slipware potter from Castle Douglas, Scotland. McAndrew writes of Wolff's potterly hospitality, "I visited Guy in Bantam in April 2011 after being in touch online for a while. He invited myself and Doug Fitch to visit while we were in the States on a demonstration tour. We were welcomed warmly and given a whirlwind tour of the great setup at his pottery. Guy demonstrated his techniques for some of his 50-pound planters and generously shared tips and hints with us fellow potters. He shared his fascinating collection of historical pots and entertained us with stories and anecdotes galore before treating us to some quick renditions on the whistle and of course the banjo.

"We left barely an hour later on our tight schedule but having had a fabulous once-in-a-lifetime visit and knowing we had met one quite extraordinary man. It was one of those stories — in the retelling you can never quite explain it in the fast frantic incredible way that would do justice to the visit or tell it how it was. You just have to go and meet him for yourself to understand." McAndrew and Fitch are both bloggers and posted throughout their trip.

A recent visitor to Guy Wolff Pottery for a "Joggleware Party" was Canadian television and film actor Rajiv Surendra. Surendra, best known for his role in *Mean Girls*, studied painting, sculpture and pottery at the Wexford School for the Arts and later at the University of Toronto.

Stopping by Wolff's rustic shop, you never know whom else you will encounter.

Wolff has four children: Ben, Sam, Christian, and Elizabeth; two of whom, Elizabeth and Ben, have become artists and one, his oldest child Ben, has become a potter. Like his father, Ben Wolff focuses on horticultural pots, he explains, because it allows him to meld the two parts of his life, his love of pottery and his love of growing things. He recalls playing in his dad's shop as a young boy, and has in his possession a pot dated 1982, which, since he was born in December of 1980, would tell us that he was about a year old when he made it. "Even though they were just dumpy kinds of little things, a couple look like candlestick holders except the hole went all the way through, he would fire them for me," Ben Wolff says. He proudly displays a small black-and-white photo of his two-year-old self at a wheel on his website. At that time, Wolff was doing stoneware and "he would take the time to glaze them and fire them in the high fire kiln. It was very cool and it's very cool to look back and see all the different glazes he was using at the time. I don't remember using any of them personally. I think he just did them for me. All I did was kind of just make the pot . . . my father and my mother were divorced I think in '86 so I spent weekends with my father and, of course, weekends for a potter is the sales time so I was always around the pottery and watching him do the business."

His brother Sam, eighteen months his junior, played in the pottery too, though in the end, he did not choose to become a potter. "Sam was interested in it too. He actually made a lot of the foot molds, you know, pottery feet. He kind of messed around with that stuff. You know ... being a potter [my dad] was busy doing his thing. You are a little kid; you want to be outside ... Dad's got to do the pottery, afterwards he would take us out to play and for ice cream ... It took me until I was in high school to really get a sense of what he was doing and a sense of appreciation for the whole thing. 'Cause when you are a child you say mommy and daddy are doing this, I want to go play, I want to go play in the dirt."

Where he also played was inside the kiln. "It's kind of hard as a child not to jump up into the kiln. I do remember hiding out in there. So we used to play in there all the time. I have pictures of myself in the kiln. It was actually fun; a little cave you can go in when it's not being fired."

Eventually, he found himself making more and more pots. He talks about the senior Wolff's teaching methods. "He definitely took an alternative approach with me and I am really grateful for it. We call it osmosis. He let me go ... and the wheel and the clay teach you and every piece is different and teaches you a whole different part that you are not realizing. He kind of did that. I'd make the pots and then we'd sit down and say okay, let's look at them, and he'd said well this one is a little too thick on the bottom or the top, or it's not even all the way up or it's this and that, and then it's like, okay let's do another one. And I'd go and make my pots." His father never said, "'Hey, you're doing something wrong.' He kind of let it happen and then afterwards we'd say the positives and the negatives about the piece, and it got me appreciating the teaching process because I was always an alternative learner. Somebody could tell me a hundred times what to do, and I'd go oh god, without doing it I [can't learn]. I always had to know by actually doing. He was very kind about that. He let me do it.

"Toward junior year of high school I made a batch of ... what we called number one, one-pound pots, and they were all different sizes, different thicknesses, that kind of thing. I came in one day a few weeks after making these one-pound pots and he said, 'Hey, your pots sold,' and I didn't even know they were for sale. I was humbled, very happy and very surprised that I had a little money in my hand from doing something that was a lot of fun. So that was my light bulb going off. So people actually liked this and they purchased it? So I was okay, this is cool. I will do this again. And I tried it again and again and it got to be whenever I got a free moment. I also did normal kind of jobs. I grew up on a dairy farm so I worked on the dairy farm in high school and I did random jobs. It takes a while to build as an artist to be where you know; I am going to focus my life . . . on art. 'Cause you know it's not always definite that something is going to happen with it. I just sort of went with it after that. I said okay, well if people like it, I am going to keep going with it.

"My father was very kind to me in a sort of teachering fashion. He wasn't, 'Go make this and make a hundred of them,' which is what some apprentices basically do. I kind of didn't treat it as an apprenticeship. He just said go for it. Have fun, kid. He really wanted me to like the whole process. He did the right thing."

Ironically, in the town of Goshen, where Ben Wolff now has his own pottery, the nineteenth-century redware potter Hervey Brooks (1779–1873), whose shop was moved to Sturbridge Village, took his ten-year-old son Isaac as an apprentice. Isaac did not care for making pots and was not a happy apprentice. The senior Brooks was likely a taskmaster to his son, as he was a taskmaster to himself. Isaac ran away to Georgia before his twentieth birthday. Sadly, Hervey wrote down in his records that Isaac owed him $133.00 for his apprenticeship! Eventually he forgave the debt.[6] Wolff might be a traditional potter in many ways, and fascinated with the old ways of working, but he is not a traditional teacher or Master Potter in his teaching methods. His philosophy stems more from the High Mowing ideology.

In 2007, Wolff began making YouTube videos of both his music and his throwing. In his throwing videos, as in his demonstrations, or when visitors come to his shop, he skillfully articulates exactly what he is doing as he is doing it. One can imagine learning to throw a large flowerpot just by watching him, and listening to him talk. "He really knows what he is doing with his hands and with the wheel. In time he's really learned how to describe that and show people," his son Ben says.

"I learned a lot from him. Not only being a potter, you also have to be a businessman. You have to make the stuff, which for a potter is kind of the easy part. Then you have to deal with running the store and how do things look in certain places. Kind of a whole different thing than just making pots. I always say that to people. Hey, making pots is the easy part. It's doing the rest that's the hard thing.

"We used to have a lot of fun together. When we made pots we would chuck clay at each other. Just father-son kind of fun stuff. Mainly we'd make pots and we also shared an interest in music together so a lot of our time was spent making pots and . . . because both wheels are in the same room, we'd look over at each other and . . . you know he would like to listen to the country-time banjo stuff and I would like to listen to jazz fusion and we'd bicker back and forth about music and then we'd have fun with the whole thing . . . We actually got to go to England together before the end of high school and checked out a few potteries."

In 1999, Ben began working on developing his own line of flowerpots and establishing his own business. He had already appeared with Wolff on the *Martha Stewart Show*. After working in the Guy Wolff Pottery on his pieces for five years, he moved to his own shop at his home in Goshen, Connecticut, around 2003.

"He's a very busy individual and has done a lot of different things in his life and his career," the younger Wolff says finally. "He's been a really good potter my whole life. I really looked up to him and I still do. He is an amazing potter."

Gardeners fortunate enough to have Wolff's pots in their possession know how spectacular a pair of fragrant rosemary topiaries planted in his white long toms look. They revel in a Hartford Pot planted with coleus and trailing Empress of India nasturtium, and perhaps a lemon-scented geranium. One of his big conservatory pots filled with Apricot Beauty tulips in the spring and hens and chicks in summer makes a stunning focal point on the terrace. Bring the old sansevieria out of its dusty corner and give it a new home in a 25-pound English pot and you will never neglect your grandmother's snake plant again. It will now make your heart stop every morning when you look at it on your way to prepare breakfast. You will want to tend it.

Wolff makes his flowerpots to be used. They are not meant to sit empty and untouched in a display cabinet like a prized teapot, though they are pretty enough for such pride of place. Peggy Cornett of Monticello keeps Wolff's pots in her home and in her office, some planted but others empty because they are so beautiful to look at.

But in Wolff's mind, they are made to hold rich crumbly earth and the roots of plants. Lined up, one inside the next on shelves in the potting shed, or stacked upside down by the potager gate, they convey expectancy and the promise of the next year's growth. Grouped together or alone as a focal point, planted, they celebrate the vegetation within their embrace. Clustered on a table, lined up on a windowsill, set singly on the floor near a cupboard, Wolff's pots make the flora residing within look its spectacular best.

Wolff's pots are especially effective because you can sense the energy of the throwing, the movement of the clay, long after they have left the wheel. They are of a size that they can hold their own in a garden of tall plants.

Entire books and specialty magazines are devoted to planting in pots, or containers as they are often referred to, full of advice on plant combinations and care and usually lots of photos. There are arguments about whether it is best to mass one type of plant, or select a complement of trailing and spikey plants. No matter, connoisseurs say that even the most plebian of garden plants is raised to a new level in one of Wolff's pots. And the most special of plants is suitably accommodated.

Joe Eck says of Wolff's pots, "We have a magnificent collection. I think we probably have the biggest collection in America of pots by Guy. And he has made all kinds of pots for us. Alpine pots and a huge pot, huge, fired in Impruneta to Guy's design, in which lives a *Xanthorrhoea quadrangulata* which is probably the rarest plant in North America, I am aware of four in the whole country, and it's truly magnificent . . . we have a display shelf of our own pots, which are not for sale, many of which are by Guy."

Martha Stewart, effusing over the "historical shapes" Wolff makes, also likes the range of sizes, "from about 2 inches in diameter to 25 inches" and "the coggle-made details."[7] Stewart has a vast collection of indoor plants, "30-year-old topiaries from Allen C. Haskell Horticulturalists," clivia, begonias, schefflera, among others that she grows at optimum conditions in her Bedford greenhouse and rotates into the rooms of her house when the plants are at peak. "Budding *Chirita* 'Aiko' . . . red-flowered *Columnea* 'Boehme' and the 'Firebird,' and the moss *Selaginella kraussiana* grow in pots made by Guy Wolff, who stamps each with 'Cantitoe Corners' [the name of her New York estate] and the year it is thrown."[8] Two Wolff conservatory pots set on pedestals and planted with large jade plants flank one of the fireplaces in her home. Stewart commissioned Wolff to make pots for her greenhouse and home using a special gray wash that his son Ben developed. "At my farm," she writes, "I am reluctant to introduce other types of pots — no red terracotta, or colored glazed pots, just cement or gray stone or Wolff pots."[9]

Garden writer and blogger (awaytogarden.com) Margaret Roach, whose most recent book is *The Backyard Parables*, appreciates that Wolff has brought the traditional shapes back. She writes, "Where would we be without Guy

Wolff? In a garden without must-have shapes like long toms or bulb pans (and ignorant of the proper names of such classic clay beauties that he thankfully rediscovered and revived)."[10]

Eck describes an episode when Wolff came to his flowerpot-rescue: "Several years ago Wayne and I were asked to deliver a lecture to the Women's Club of Fredericksburg, Virginia so we went down there and there were all these elegant women. And we were asked to do a demonstration as well as a lecture and asked only seven days before the event. So we called Guy and we said, 'Guy, we've got to do this demonstration. Could you provide us with plantation pots from Virginia that we could plant in front of all these ladies and then sell for outrageous sums of money?' and he said, 'Of course I can. I know all those pots.' And so we got pots from Monticello and Mount Vernon and from Madison's house, Monroe's house — all these gorgeous reproduction eighteenth-century pots and we did show them and give their history and plant them and they were auctioned off for vast sums of money, I mean $500, $600, $700 a pot for the charities that these ladies supported. That he did it and he did it so quickly and he got them down to us, he's just a marvel."

A pot of pelargoniums welcomes visitors to Wolff's pottery.

Wolff's own garden — or more correctly, his wife Erica Warnock's, for she is the artist and plantswoman behind it — begins with sprawling forsythia bushes that spill down the slope from the shop to the edge of the road. In spring, he likes to clip a branch or two of the chromium yellow flowers and place them in one of his pots, suggesting both the formality of a Japanese arrangement and the generosity of country gardens that have grown forsythia throughout New England for hundreds of years. Ascending the crunchy gravel drive, you see the red pottery shop on your left, and on your right an enormous low-cut stump, with one of Wolff's pots thickly planted with bright red geraniums, pale yellow snapdragons, and a spikey burgundy cordyline. The lawn is dappled with shade from ancient maple and oak, a shagbark hickory or two. Granite boulders erupt from the grass, remnants of the glacial era. The house, a Cape, sits at the crest of the hill

The front door and
granite stepping stone of
Wolff's home are flanked
by two of his pots.

Pink astilbe billow
from a Wolff
flowerpot, the
centerpiece of the
main garden.

looking as if it has always been there. A fieldstone walk leads to the front door, which is flanked by two large pots.

In front, under outstretched branches of a venerable maple, are a bench and chair and the "Calder table." Wolff explains that one night during one of the famously exuberant dinner parties, "Calder drew a picture on the table that my mother found too rude for her mother to see, and so [the next morning she] sanded it clean."

Today, one of Wolff's large flowerpots sits on the table, planted with a lusty rex begonia, so thick with crinkled leaves that the rim of the pot is nearly invisible. Pot and plant appear to have lived happily together for some time, as evidenced by the moss that grows on the side of the pot. A smaller pot on a pedestal sits beside the bench.

The main part of the garden is just steps beyond. You can sit on the bench and gaze at it, perhaps watch for butterflies, or take the short walk over. You enter between two pots planted with pink astilbe, and wander the circular gravel path, slowly so that you can see all there is to see. The raised beds are abundantly planted with multiple varieties of hosta, iris, echinacea, steely blue *Echinops ritro*, old-fashioned phlox, daisies, begonia, deep blue balloon flowers, a few deep pink stargazer lilies, and *Nicotiana alata*. In the center, partially hidden by the plants, a huge sleeping mound of a boulder rests. Set atop it is another of Wolff's large flowerpots, this one planted with blowsy pink astilbe fringed with dusty miller and licorice, to echo the two pots at the garden's entrance.

Between this garden and the house is a smaller one. Here there is a cluster of pots in front, and another cluster on an erupting glacial rock. One pot boasts what seems to be the world's tallest cleome, her spidery pink head regally looking down upon the rest of the garden. Oh how happy her feet must be, ensconced in Wolff's magnificent pot!

Beyond are traditional wooden raised beds, again thickly planted, and beyond again, a silvered garden shed. There are flowers, daisies and black-eyed Susans, along the side of the house.

Wolff continues to make pots by hand, alone in his shop. The Metropolitan Museum of Art recently asked him to design pots to celebrate the seventy-fifth anniversary of The Cloisters Museum and Garden in Fort Tryon Park overlooking the Hudson River. The Cloisters showcases the Met's collection of medieval art and architecture from the ninth to the sixteenth centuries, and features enclosed medieval gardens with raised wattle beds of herbs and spices and heirloom trees, shrubs, and flowers. This is just the sort of project that delights Wolff.

There are three types of potters: those who are enthralled with the firing process, subjecting their work to the risks of flames or manipulating their kiln temperatures to rise and fall for particular effect; those who are fascinated with glazes and focus on the intricacies of glaze chemistry and all that can be achieved in the glazing process; and the mud potters who are in love with clay and the process of making, and value form above all else. Wolff is a mud potter. He has brought his deep commitment to form to the level of high art and imbued his pots with history and purpose and, most important to him, beauty. Eschewing the postmodernist trends in ceramics of the past two decades, he embraces beauty above all else. His flowerpots are not political statements except in the broadest humanist sense.

Peale pot in white clay with the charming roped rim that Wolff makes with his handmade three-dimensional coggle; 4 pounds, 2012.

Wolff stamps or coggles the pots that he makes with "G. Wolff," and usually adds the date and weight. He also hand-signs the pots on the bottom. All pots with "G. Wolff" were made by him on his wheel between 1971 when he opened shop and the present. Pots stamped "G. Wolff Pottery" were made in his shop, under his supervision, and fired by him. Other pots, such as those stamped "Guy Wolff," "G. Wolff & Co.," and "Guywolff Greenhouse" were made in the Guilds.

Potting is physically demanding. As the years progress, it takes a toll on the potter's body, yet a remarkable number of potters make their work late in life. Lucie Rie threw pots until she was 88. Karen Karnes (who knew Wolff's father), and Val Cushing, in their eighties, are still potting. Wolff, in his early sixties, is making some of his best work. He continues to explore and discover and to work hard at his craft. He continues to hold his father's words, "Tradition is not a form to be imitated, but the discipline that gives integrity to the new," as his creed. His father, the Abstract Expressionist artist Robert Jay Wolff, who once misunderstood his son's endeavors as "shop keeping," would be proud of Guy Wolff, the Master Potter and artist.

First, I want to thank Larry Dorfman who proposed the original idea. Thank you, Larry. And a huge thank you to all the people who gave me their time and thoughtful attention for interviews, emails, questions, comments, and phone calls: Peter Jackson who has been an enormous help, especially with the history of the Guy Wolff Guilds; Peter Arango, Peggy Cornett, Val Cushing, Joe Eck, Steve Fischer, Sharry Stevens-Grudin, Mrs. Karl, Simon Leach, Tovah Martin, Hannah McAndrews, Todd Piker, Margaret Roach, Mara Seibert, Susan Tamulevich, Gordon Titcomb, Abby, Ethan and Chrissy Weisgard, and Ben Wolff. Thanks too to Judy Doyle for her close read of the manuscript and to Lary Bloom who encourages me to write. And thanks go to Mary Bisbee-Beek and Roger Williams who found such a good home for the book. A special thanks to Guy Wolff for being such a cooperative subject, even when I pried and pestered. And a huge thank you to Joe Szalay who worked as hard on the project as I did, and who took the beautiful photos that grace the book.

Three 4-pound pots with very different rims: from left to right, Maryland, Peale, and Galena.

CHAPTER ONE. GUY WOLFF

1. John Windsor, "None of That Fancy Stuff," *The Independent On Sunday*, Saturday, November 18, 1995, U.K.

2. Ibid.

3. John Anderson, *Making Pottery*, Broughton Skipton, U.K.: Dalesman Publishing, 1999.

CHAPTER TWO. FLOWERPOTS THROUGH THE MILLENNIA

1. Suzanne Staubach, *Clay*, New York: Penguin, 2005, pp. 160–79.

2. Linda Farrar, *Ancient Roman Gardens*, Thrupp, Stroud, Gloucestershire, U.K.: Sutton Publishing, 1998, p. 18; see also Pliny the Elder, *Natural History*, XIX, 19, 51.

3. Anthony Huxley, *An Illustrated History of Gardening*, London: Paddington Press, 1978, p. 64.

4. Cato, *Martial* (XI.19.1, 2).

5. Anne Wilkinson, *The Passion for Pelargoniums*, Thrupp Stroud, Gloucestershire: Sutton Publishing, 2007, p. 18.

6. H. Peter Loewer, *Jefferson's Garden*, Mechanicsburg, PA: Stackpole Books, 2004.

7. Susan Condor, *The Complete Geranium*, New York: Clarkson Potter, 1992, p. 8.

CHAPTER THREE. EARLY YEARS AND INFLUENCES

1. Email conversation with Guy Wolff, January 29, 2012.

2. Pedro E. Guerraro, *Calder at Home*, New York: Stewart, Tabori & Chang, 1998, pp. 32–33.

3. Robert Jay Wolff, edited by Dina Wolff, *The Man from Highbelow*, Durango, CO: Authentic, p. 92.

4. http://www.americanabstractartists.org/

5. Howard Singerman, *Art Subjects: Making Artists in the American University*, Berkeley: University of California Press, 1999, p. 133.

6. *New York Times*, November 21, 1978.

7. http://www.highmowing.org/page.cfm?p=518 (accessed 2/24/2012).

8. http://www.whywaldorfworks.org/02_W_Education/index.asp (accessed 2/25/2012).

9. Margaret Carney, *Charles Fergus Binns: The Father of American Studio Ceramics*, New York: Hudson Hills Press, 1998.

10. Val Cushing, email to the author, January 10, 2012.

11. Bernard Leach, *A Potter's Book*, Levittown, NY: Transatlantic Arts, 1970, pp. 11–12.

12. Jesse Salisbury, "Sweezy, former Wilton 'national treasure,'" Obituaries, *Nashua Telegraph*, February 14, 2010.

13. Charlotte Vestal Brown, "175 Years of Pottery by the Owen/Owens," http://www.ncarts.org/press_release.cfm?ID=442, March 13, 2012.

14. Nancy Sweezy, *Raised in Clay: The Southern Pottery Tradition*, Washington, DC: Smithsonian Institution Press for the Office of Folklife Programs, 1984, p. 211.

15. Ibid., 211–213.

CHAPTER FOUR. SEEKING THE OLD MASTERS

1. Bernard Leach, *Hamada Potter*, Tokyo and New York: Kodansha International, [1975] 1990, p. 131.

CHAPTER FIVE. SETTING UP SHOP

1. "Eszter Haraszky, Designer, 74," Obituaries, *New York Times*, December 1, 1994.

INDEX

Page numbers in *italics* refer to the illustrations.
Guy Wolff is abbreviated as G W.